Learn
DEWEY
DECIMAL
CLASSIFICATION

(Edition 23)

International Edition

Lynn Farkas

TotalRecall Publications, Inc..
1103 Middlecreek
Friendswood, Texas 77546
281-992-3131   281-482-5390 Fax
www.totalrecallpress.com

ISBN: 9978-1-59095-436-2
UPC: 6-43977-44360-1
Printed in the United States of America with simultaneous printing in Australia, Canada, and United Kingdom.

INTERNATIONA LEDITION, 2015
1   2   3   4   5   6   7   8   9   10

Library of Congress Control Number: 2015941363

TABLE OF CONTENTS

Acknowledgement

Thanks to Mary Mortimer, who wrote *Learn Dewey Decimal Classification* for DDC21 and DDC22, and who kindly allowed her text to form the basis of this DDC23 upgrade.

PREFACE

This book covers the skills necessary for a classifier using Dewey Decimal Classification in a library or other information agency, whether at a professional or a paraprofessional level. It is equally suitable for use by librarianship students in universities, and others who are studying classification by themselves, either with a specific goal or as part of their continuing professional development. Since most collections are organized according to a library classification scheme, and Dewey Decimal Classification is widely used, it is important for all library students and most library staff to be familiar with at least the basics.

Throughout the book you will find exercises to practice and test your skills, and quizzes to test your understanding. There are answers for self-checking at the back of the book. You may not always agree completely with the answers given, and it is useful to check them with a teacher or experienced classifier. Despite the best efforts of the editors of DDC to standardize the allocation of numbers, there is often room for more than one interpretation or emphasis.

Note on Spelling and Capitalization

This edition is designed for use in North America, Europe and Australasia, across countries that employ different spelling conventions for English words. For consistency, American spelling has been adopted for the text. However, to accommodate those used to different conventions, both English and American spellings have been used in the exercises.

Titles included in the text are capitalized according to standard library cataloging practice – that is, apart from names, only the first word of the title has a capital letter. This is intended to accustom library students and staff to this style.

CHAPTER ONE
Introduction to Classification

Introduction
A classification scheme organizes subjects systematically and shows their relationships.

 EXERCISE 1.1
Write down some examples of classification other than library classification:

Library Classification
The basic principle of library classification is to group the items on the shelves according to their subject content, or sometimes literary or bibliographic form.

Resources that are used together should be shelved together.

Literary warrant (i.e., the volume of material that has been created, or is likely to be created, on any topic) should be a primary factor in formulating a classification scheme. The Library of Congress Classification scheme is heavily based on this idea, since it was developed using the material actually held in the Library of Congress when the scheme was being developed.

Purposes of Library Classification
Library classification schemes serve to
- bring related items together in a helpful sequence
- provide formal orderly access to the shelves either through a direct search of the shelves (browsing) or via the catalog
- enable easy reshelving of library materials
- provide an order for the classified catalog.

Types of Classification

Enumerative classification attempts to spell out (enumerate) all the single and composite subject concepts required –

> e.g., Library of Congress Classification, Dewey Decimal Classification (to a lesser extent).

Synthetic classification, also called faceted classification, lists numbers for single concepts, and allows the classifier to construct (synthesize) numbers for composite subjects –

> e.g., Colon Classification, Universal Decimal Classification, some features of DDC.

Hierarchical classification is based on the division of subjects from the most general to the most specific –

> e.g., Dewey Decimal Classification, Library of Congress Classification (to a much lesser extent).

Features of a Classification Scheme

Library classification schemes generally have the following features:
- schedules
- notation
- index
- number building.

Schedules

The schedules are the printed, enumerated classes, divisions etc. of the scheme, arranged in number order. Schedules range from fairly sparse to extremely detailed. In general, the more enumerative the scheme, the more detailed the schedules; the more synthetic, the slimmer the schedules.

The Dewey Decimal Classification schedules are much shorter than the Library of Congress Classification schedules, since DDC relies more on number building, whereas LCC lists more of its numbers.

In addition, schedules usually have:
- a generalities class
- form classes
- form divisions.

The generalities class is used for very general topics, and comprehensive combinations of topics – e.g., current affairs, general encyclopedias.

Form classes are used for literature. That is, items are grouped not according to subject, but according to the literary form – poetry, drama, prose, etc. – in which they are written. These classes also include literary criticism.

Form divisions are used for resources on any subject that are presented in a particular bibliographic form—e.g., dictionary, periodical.

Notation

The notation of a classification scheme is the series of symbols that stand for the classes, subclasses, divisions and subdivisions of classes.

Notation is used to
- indicate a subject or topic
- show its relationship to a class
- provide a sequential order for arrangement.

Pure notation is the use of only one type of symbol, such as numbers—
 e.g., Dewey Decimal Classification 342.569.

Mixed notation is the use of more than one type of symbol, such as numbers and letters—
 e.g., Library of Congress Classification TK51011.H37 1994.

Good notation should
- convey order clearly and automatically
- be as brief and simple as possible
- be easy to say, write and remember
- be flexible, allowing insertion at any point without dislocating the sequence
- facilitate the use of mnemonics (memory aids).

Index

The index is the alphabetical list of the terms used in the schedules, together with the corresponding notation. It provides access to the schedules. It should include, as far as possible, all synonyms for the term, and a breakdown of parts of the subject.

There are two types of index:
- specific – with only one entry for each topic mentioned in the schedules
- relative – enumerating all topics and synonyms, and showing the relation of each topic to all the disciplines in which it is found.

Number Building

This is the ability of the scheme to allow the construction of notation to include items not specifically mentioned in the schedules.

Criteria of a Successful Classification Scheme
- It should create an order convenient to the user – the main purpose of classification.
- It should be as complete as possible, covering the whole field of knowledge.
- It should proceed from the general to the specific.
- It should be evenly apportioned, so that subjects of equal importance have roughly equivalent space in the schedules.
- It should have: – generalities and form classes
  – form and geographical divisions
  – effective notation
  – an alphabetical index.

- It should be able to accommodate new notation as knowledge expands—e.g., computers, environmental issues.
- The terms must be clear and easy to understand, accompanied where necessary by full definitions, the scope of headings and notes to guide the classifier.
- It should be presented in a form that is easy to consult, and enables the user to grasp the structure.
- It must be revised frequently, to keep up with new knowledge, new interpretations and new emphases in the presentation of knowledge.

 EXERCISE 1.2

On a large sheet of paper, create a plan of a zoo to house the following animals. Your plan must show some logical system for grouping the animals, although how you do this is up to you.

alligator	antelope	bison	black swan	brown bear	camel

cape hunting dog   cheetah   cockatoo   crocodile   deer   dingo

echidna   elephant   emu   frilled-neck lizard   giraffe   goanna

hippopotamus   ibis   kangaroo   koala   kookaburra   leopard

lion   monkey   mountain goat   orang-utan   ostrich

Pacific black duck   panther   pelican   platypus   polar bear

quokka   rosella   snake   tiger   tortoise   water buffalo

white rhinoceros   wolf   wombat   zebra

The Needs of the User

A library's classification policy needs to take account of its users and their needs. For example, many public library users regard biographies as a 'good read', and are less concerned with the specialization of a famous person than with the interesting life he or she has led. So public libraries are likely to house their biographies together, using the number for general biography, or even the simple location symbol 'B'. A medical library, on the other hand, is more likely to classify the biographies of medical researchers with the diseases or treatments they have spent much of their lives studying.

How closely a resource is classified should also take a library's users into account. A library that has only a few books about bridges does not need to differentiate between concrete bridges, wooden bridges, metal bridges and so on. However an engineering library with a large collection of books about bridges may decide to classify them very specifically, to assist users to find exactly what they want.

A library may supply its catalogers with a list of particular numbers (e.g., for literature) or a statement of general policy (e.g., no more than 8 digits after the decimal point). If the policy is to shorten numbers, the classifier must take care that the number is not reduced arbitrarily, but is still a meaningful number within the classification scheme.

When libraries use another source as the basis for their records (copy cataloging), they need to ensure that the classification number is consistent with their own cataloging and classification policies. This requires familiarity with the policies as well as the classification scheme.

Individual catalogers also make judgments about classification in relation to the library's users, in the same way as other aspects of cataloging take them into account.

Different Sequences

A library usually has several sequences of materials in its collection. These can include fiction, non-fiction books for loan, reference works (not for loan), periodicals, children's books, audiovisual materials (which may be divided into different formats—e.g., DVDs, compact discs) and so on.

Fiction is usually indicated by the location symbol 'F', and arranged alphabetically by author's surname. Periodicals are sometimes classified, using the same scheme as the main collection, and sometimes arranged alphabetically by title.

Other parts of the collection are either classified, using the same classification scheme, or arranged alphabetically or by their own number (e.g., standards) within their sequence. When a library acquires material in a new format, a decision is made about whether to integrate the material into an existing sequence or house the material separately. If a new sequence is established, a new location and the basis for organising the material will also be decided.

REVISION QUIZ 1.3

Use the following questions to revise your understanding of library classification. You do not need to write down the answers.

1. Give 3 reasons for classifying a library collection.

2. What is the difference between enumerative and synthetic classification? Give examples.

3. In what order are classification schedules arranged? Why?

4. What is number building? Why is it a desirable feature of a classification scheme?

5. What is hierarchical classification? How does it work?

6. Why should a library consider the nature of its client group when it classifies its material?

CHAPTER TWO
Introduction to Dewey Decimal Classification

Introduction

The Dewey Decimal Classification was developed by Melvil Dewey between 1873 and 1876, when the first edition was published anonymously under the title *A classification and subject index for cataloguing and arranging the books and pamphlets of a library*. At that time, libraries used 'fixed location' to classify books – that is, the books were kept in a fixed physical space in the library, and numbered according to their room, tier and shelf. They therefore had to be reclassified whenever the library grew beyond its shelving capacity. Dewey's invention of relative location – numbering books according to their intellectual content – formed the basis of library classification as we know it today.

The first edition of his scheme was a 44-page pamphlet, and was based on Dewey's view of the world of knowledge that is still used today. The scheme was criticised at the time for being too lengthy. It was, however, an immediate success, and in its succeeding editions has become the most widely used classification scheme, being translated into many languages.

The Dewey editorial office has been located in the Dewey Section (formerly Decimal Classification Division) of the Library of Congress since 1923. The Section allocates over 90,000 numbers annually to resources cataloged by the Library of Congress. The editor and assistant editors responsible for updating DDC work closely with classification specialists, so that they can detect trends in the published literature.

The Decimal Classification Editorial Policy Committee (EPC) is a ten-member international board that advises the editors of DDC on the development of the Classification. EPC represents the interests of all DDC users, and responds to suggestions from many countries and different types of libraries.

DDC is now in its 23rd edition, published in 2011 by OCLC. In recent times it has been revised every 7 to 10 years. There is also an abridged version, with the 15th abridged edition published in 2012.

In 1993 a DOS version of the 20th edition, called *Electronic Dewey,* was published on CD-ROM. *Dewey for Windows,* a Microsoft Windows®-based version of *Electronic Dewey*, was published at the same time as Edition 21 in 1996. These have now been replaced by *WebDewey* and *Abridged WebDewey*, electronic versions of the DDC databases with enhanced interfaces, accessible via the Internet and updated continuously.

New numbers and changes to the DDC are posted on the website (www.oclc.org/dewey). The DDC website also contains up-to-date information about the DDC, DDC products and services, and DDC licensing.

Format of DDC
The 23rd edition of DDC is published in 4 volumes with almost 4000 pages:

Volume 1	Introduction, Glossary, Manual, and Tables 1–6
Volume 2	Schedules 000–599
Volume 3	Schedules 600–999
Volume 4	Relative Index

General Characteristics of DDC

Hierarchy

DDC is a hierarchical classification, proceeding from the general to the specific in terms of discipline and subject relationships.

The basic arrangement is by discipline, and the same subject may appear in a number of disciplines. The various aspects of a subject are brought together by the Relative Index.

There are 10 classes (see the First Summary, in volume 2 of the schedules). Each of the classes from 100 to 900 represents a broad discipline or group of disciplines. The 000 class contains general subjects that are not necessarily related disciplines—e.g., newspapers, encyclopedias, computers and library science.

Each class has 10 divisions, represented by the second digit of the notation (see the Second Summary, in volume 2 of the schedules).

Each division has 10 sections, represented by the third digit of the notation (see the Third Summary, in volume 2 of the schedules).

This hierarchical structure is continued and incorporated in the notation, which is lengthened by one digit for each more specific aspect of the subject.

  For example,

600	Technology (Applied sciences)
640	Home and family management
646	Sewing, clothing, management of personal and family life
646.7	Management of personal and family life
646.72	Care of hair, face, skin, nails
646.724	Care of hair
646.7248	Wigs

Number Building

Over 40,000 numbers are listed in the schedules. However DDC also uses number building to expand the classification scheme, and create even more specific numbers.

Numbers are constructed by taking a number from the schedules, and adding to it digits from Tables 1–6, or from another part of the schedules.

Tables 1 to 6 (also called the auxiliary tables) allow the classifier to make numbers more specific in relation to time periods, places, types of persons, language, literary form and so on. For example, the geographic aspect of almost any subject can be included by adding one or more digits from Table 2 (Geographic Areas, Historical Periods, Biography).

Internal tables in the schedules enable aspects, or facets, of one subject to be applied to another subject. For example, many aspects of particular animals and animal groups are listed only once in the schedules, but can be added to any animals with classification numbers between 592 and 599.

The Relative Index

No one class can cover all the aspects of a subject. For many subjects, different aspects are located in different classes. The Relative Index brings together (relates) the different aspects of a topic and the different classes where they are to be found. Here are some of the entries for the topic Metals:

Metals	669
applied nutrition	613.285 1
architectural construction	721.044 7
architectural decoration	729.6
biochemistry	572.51
humans	612.015 24
building construction	693.7
building materials	691.8
chemistry	546.3
decorative arts	739
dowsing	133.323 3
economic geology	553.4
foundation materials	624.153 6
handicrafts	745.56
human toxicology	615.925 3
materials science	620.16
metabolism	572.514
human physiology	612.392 4
metallography	669.95
military resources	355.242
mineralogy	549.23
mining	622.34

and so on.

Notation

DDC notation uses only Arabic numerals. Use of only one type of symbol is called pure notation. All numbers contain at least three digits. Where more than 3 digits are needed, a decimal point follows the third digit.

In the print version of DDC, numbers are written in groups of three digits, with a space between each group—e.g., 344.063 635 1. This is only done to make remembering and writing numbers easier.

Some notation is mnemonic – that is, it is easy to remember some numbers because they are used consistently for a particular topic or subtopic. For example, '9' often represents geography or history, whether in the class 900 History & geography, or in the standard subdivision –09 History, geographic treatment, biography.

Segmentation and Reduction

DDC allows for numbers to be reduced if the library requires a shorter number. Dividing a number into meaningful parts so that an abbreviated number can be used in the library is known as segmentation. Some copy cataloging sources, including cataloging-in-publication, show the segmentation of DDC numbers, to enable shorter numbers to be identified easily. Segmentation is often indicated in DDC numbers by using apostrophes to show where a meaningful number can be ended. For example, 025.4'31 means that 025.431 is the complete number, but 025.4 is also correct (although less specific).

If segmentation is not shown, you need to consult the schedules to find a meaningful reduced number. As you develop familiarity with DDC, reduction will often be possible without needing to consult the schedules.

Order of DDC Numbers

DDC numbers are arranged in decimal number order. In other words, after the decimal point, look at each decimal place one at a time, and put those numbers in order. Unless they are the same, you will not need to look at the next place.

 For example,

      3 4 8 . 0 0 3
      3 4 8 . 0 1
      3 4 8 . 0 2
      3 4 8 . 0 2 2
      3 4 8 . 0 4
      3 4 8 . 0 4 1
      3 4 8 . 6
      3 4 8 . 7 4
      3 4 8 . 7 4 4

EXERCISE 2.1

Check the order of these numbers, and correct them where necessary:

616	361
616.11	361.1
616.122	361.02
616.123	361.04
616.125	361.003
616.1237	361.103
616.09	361.2
616.24	361.3
616.201	361.23
616.241	361.301
616.244	361.32
616.200435	361.322
616.240083	361.37
615.954	361.32205
617.44	361.3703
617.80083	361.37025
617.08	361.3205
617.0083	361.320994
616.2009	

Key Points:

Advantages of DDC

1. DDC was the first to use the concept of relative location to organize materials on the shelf.
2. The pure notation (i.e., all Arabic numbers) is recognized internationally.
3. The straightforward numerical sequence facilitates filing and shelving.
4. The Relative Index brings together different aspects of the same subject that are scattered in different disciplines.
5. The hierarchical notation expresses relationships between and among class numbers.
6. The decimal system theoretically enables infinite expansion and subdivision.
7. The mnemonic notation helps users to memorize and recognize class numbers.
8. Periodic revision keeps it up-to-date.

Disadvantages of DDC

1. Its Anglo-American bias is evident in its emphasis on:
    *   American, English and European language in the 400s, literature in the 800s and history in the 900s,
    *   Protestantism and Christianity in the 200s (although the 23rd edition has expanded its coverage of some non-Christian religions).
2. Some related disciplines are separated—e.g., 400 / 800;   300 / 900.

3.   Some subjects are not very comfortably placed:
- Library science in 000
- Psychology as part of Philosophy in 100
- Sports and amusements in 700.

4.   In the 800s, literary works by the same author are scattered according to form–e.g., Shakespeare's poems are separated from his plays.

5.   Decimal numbering limits its capacity for accommodating subjects on the same level– there can only be 9 divisions (+ 1 general division).

6.   Different rates of growth of some disciplines have resulted in an uneven structure–e.g., 300 and 600 are particularly overcrowded.

7.   Although theoretically expansion is infinite, it doesn't allow infinite insertion between related numbers—e.g., between 610 and 619.

8.   Specificity results in long numbers that can be awkward for shelving and on spine labels.

9.   Altering numbers because of a new edition creates practical problems in libraries–e.g., the need for reclassification, relabelling, and reshelving.

REVISION QUIZ 2.2

Use the following questions to revise your understanding of the structure of DDC. You do not need to write down the answers.

1.   Describe the overall structure of Dewey Decimal Classification.

2.   Why is the Relative Index so called?

3.   Give 3 advantages of DDC.

4.   Give 3 disadvantages of DDC.

CHAPTER THREE
Principles of Classifying With DDC

Introduction
The Introduction in Volume 1 outlines a number of principles of classifying with Dewey Decimal Classification. The most significant principles are summarized here. It is important to read the Introduction, and to refer to it from time to time.

Basic Principles of Classification
1. Place a work where it will be most useful.
    Classification must take into account the needs of the users, for example in how specific a number is given

2. Class a work according to the author's intent.
    e.g., a book of drawings of dogs may be classified with drawing or with dogs, depending on whether it is intended as a guide to drawing dogs or to identifying breeds of dog

3. Class by subject, then by form, except in works of the imagination.
    e.g., an encyclopedia of art is classified with art rather than general encyclopedias

4. In works of the imagination, class by original language, then literary form, rather than by subject.
    e.g., an anthology of English-language poems about the weather is classified with English poetry, not meteorology; a French translation of an English play is classified with English drama

5. Class a work in the most specific area possible.
    e.g., a DVD about violins is classified at the specific number for violins rather than the more general number for stringed instruments

6. Class a work that covers two or more subjects with the one that receives fuller treatment.
    e.g., a book about airplanes with a chapter on space shuttles is classified at the number for aircraft

7. If a work includes two subjects in the same discipline that receive equal treatment, and are not used to introduce or explain one another, class the work with the subject coming first in the schedules.
    e.g., a film on physics and chemistry is classified at the number for physics, since it comes first in the schedules

8.   If a work treats two aspects of a subject in different disciplines, class the work at the interdisciplinary number if one is given (provided the work contains significant material on that discipline).
      e.g., a thesis on music in education and in religious worship is classified at the interdisciplinary number for music

9.   If no emphasis is apparent, class a work on three or more subjects that are all subdivisions of a broader subject with the first higher number that includes them all.
      e.g., a journal on arithmetic, algebra and calculus is classified at the number for mathematics

10.   Class a work on three or more subjects in different disciplines in the generalities class.
      e.g., a book on history, geography, economics and politics is classified in 000 Generalities

11.   Class biographies, autobiographies, diaries and reminiscences either with specific disciplines or together in a general biography section.
      e.g., in a technical library, the life of an inventor is classified with the invention, whereas in a public library all kinds of biographies may be located together

12.   In general, class a work first by subject then by geographical location.
      e.g., a resource on German architecture is classified first at the number for architecture

13.   When there is a further subdivision and there is a choice between subject and geographical location, choose the subject first.
      e.g., for a resource on the architecture of German school buildings, the number for the architecture of school buildings is assigned before adding a number for Germany

14.   If a subject acts upon another subject, class it under the subject that is acted upon.
      e.g., an e-book on decoration in architecture is classified in architecture

15.   If a work has been treated from a particular standpoint, class in the subject unless it has been considerably altered.
      e.g., mathematics for plumbers is classified at the number for mathematics

16.   Works on topics 'with special reference to' are classed under the more specific subject.
      e.g., a documentary on contagious diseases, especially leprosy, is classified at the number for leprosy

17.   When a subject has no stated place in the classification scheme, use the number of the subject to which it is most closely related.
      e.g., for Internet advertising via smartphones, use the number for advertising in digital media

18. When two headings clash, make a decision as to which is to prevail, and be consistent in its use.

    e.g., political and armed struggle in Ireland – decide between politics and military science in Ireland

19. When several numbers have been found for the work in hand, and each seems as good as the next, use the following 'table of last resort' as a guideline in the absence of any other rule:

    (1) Kinds of things
    (2) Parts of things
    (3) Materials from which things, kinds, or parts are made
    (4) Properties of things, kinds, parts, or materials
    (5) Processes within things, kinds, parts, or materials
    (6) Operations upon things, kinds, parts, or materials
    (7) Instrumentalities for performing such operations

    e.g., surveillance by border patrols could be classed in either 363.285 Border patrols, or 363.232 Patrol and surveillance. Choose 363.285 since border patrols are a kind of police service, while patrol and surveillance are processes performed by police services

20. Works pro and con a subject go together at the subject.

    e.g., material for and against voluntary euthanasia must be found at the same number – this reinforces the principle of objectivity in the library's collection

21. Avoid placings that are in the nature of criticism.

    e.g., do not place resources on prostitution with law or ethics unless they specifically treat legal or ethical issues

22. Always have a reason for your placing of a work.

    You need to know why you assign a particular number

23. Record all decisions.

    Decisions about classification numbers may need to be referred to, to ensure consistent placement of similar resources

24. Read the introduction to the classification scheme.

    It is important to understand the approach of those who have created and maintain the scheme

25. Check the number in the shelflist or catalog.

    This will assist in placing similar resources together

EXERCISE 3.1

Using the above guidelines, name the subject where you would classify the following titles, and which principle(s) you have used:

1. Epilepsy is not a dirty word   _____

2. Conversations on drawing, painting and sculpture   _____

3. Astrology and your child   _____

4. The Daily Telegraph fishing and boating guide   _____

5. Society in view: a graphic atlas for the social sciences   _____

6. Kiiroi nezumi, by H. Inoue (Japanese novelist, 1946–)   _____

7. Enquire within for everything   _____

8. Around Seattle : including the shores of Puget Sound (more than half the text deals with Seattle)   _____

9. Words on wine: quotations from world literature   _____

10. Seven cities of Italy   _____

11. The authority and relevance of the Bible in the modern world   _____

12. Inflation in Bolivia   _____

13. Apples and pears   _____

14. The story of the apple   _____

15. Apples, oranges, pears and plums   _____

16. Peaches, nectarines and plums   _____

17. Mechanical harvesting of berry fruit   _____

18. Treasury of Scottish landscape painting   _____

19. Australian and New Zealand guide to compost gardening, with detailed instructions on composting   _____

20. Keeping faith alive today   _____

Classifying with DDC

"Classifying a work with the DDC requires determining the subject, the disciplinary focus, and, if applicable, the approach or form" – *DDC Introduction, paragraph 5.1.*

Determining the Subject

The classifier needs to examine the item in hand. This examination includes:

- the title – sometimes not very helpful
- the rest of the title information – often much more informative
- the table of contents / chapter headings / subheadings – good indications of the main topics
- the preface / introduction / foreword – usually state the author's purpose
- scanning the text – confirms or alters your ideas about the subject
- cataloging-in-publication – can be useful, but take care, since it was prepared before the resource was published.

If you are unfamiliar with the subject, you may need to consult a subject expert. Very occasionally it is necessary to consult reference works or reviews.

Determining the Discipline

Once you have decided on the subject of the resource, choose the discipline in which the subject belongs. For example, if the resource is about horses, decide whether it belongs with zoology – natural sciences (if it is about the anatomy and physiology of horses), or animal husbandry – applied sciences (if it is about breeding and rearing horses).

Then you can choose to look first in the Relative Index, or go straight to the schedules. Many experienced classifiers turn to the schedules, but while you are learning the structure of DDC, it is usually easier to look up the term(s) in the Index. The Index offers several numbers for most terms, so your decision about the discipline is important in helping to identify the most likely number. It is still necessary to check the number in the schedules before making the final decision.

 Never use a classification number direct from the Index without also checking the schedules.

Broad and Close Classification

Broad classification uses the main divisions and subdivisions of a scheme without breaking down into narrower concepts.

Close classification means classifying each resource as specifically as possible, using all available subdivisions in the classification scheme.

EXERCISE 3.2

Is the classification of each subject broad or close?

Subject	Classification Heading	Broad / Close
Physical therapies	Physical therapies	_____
Marital relationship	Marriage & family	_____
Rome's history	History of Italy	_____
Marriage counselling	Family problems & services	_____
Business law	Law	_____
Modern French Bible	Modern language Bibles	_____
The Shakers (religious group)	Adherents of religious groups	_____
Blood	Blood	_____
Banking in Egypt	Egyptian banks and banking	_____
Christian Church's views on sex, marriage & family	Christian attitudes on sex, marriage & family	_____

Citation and Preference Order

When a number of aspects (or characteristics or facets) of a subject (e.g., age, gender, place, historical period) need to be considered, citation and preference order give guidelines as to the order in which to deal with them.

Citation Order

Citation order applies when you are allowed to add two or more characteristics when building a number. It is the order in which you are instructed to add aspects of the subject, and is clearly specified in the number-building instruction.

For example,

> 909.04 History with respect to ethnic and national groups
> .041–.049 Specific ethnic and national groups
>> Add to base number 909.04 notation 1–9 from Table 5, e.g., world history of Jews 909.04924; then add 0 and to the result add the numbers following 909 in 909.1–909.8, e.g., world history of Jews in 18th century 909.0492407

In other words, the citation order is

world history + specific ethnic or national group + historical period.

Preference Order

When a subject has more than one characteristic, but the rules allow only one to be added, the classifier needs to choose. Preference notes provide guidance, for example,

> *Except where instructed otherwise, give preference to ethnic group over nationality, e.g. ...*

There are also preference tables:

 For example,

> 371.91   [Education of] students with physical disabilities
>
> Unless other instructions are given, observe the following table of preference:

Students with linguistic disorders	371.914
Students with mobility impairments	371.916
Students with blindness & visual impairments	371.911
Students with hearing impairments	371.912

That is, a resource about the education of blind and deaf students is classified at 371.911, not 371.912. However, the education of paraplegic blind students is classified at 371.916, not 371.911.

Notes indicating citation and preference order can be found throughout the schedules and tables. It is very important to read all instructions in the section(s) you are consulting.

Call Numbers

A call number is the number on a library item that shows where it is located. It usually consists of a classification number, a book number and often a location symbol.

 For example,

REF	location symbol
636.7	classification number
HEW	book number

The classification number indicates the subject of the item, and sometimes also the bibliographic form.

The book number relates to the item itself. It is usually taken from the author or the title of the item.

The location symbol shows where the item is housed. For example, a reference work may have 'R' or 'REF'; an audiovisual item may have 'AV'. Location symbols may also indicate a branch of a library system.

Classification Numbers

In DDC, the classification number is taken straight from the schedules, or built according to instructions. It can be used with any type of book number. Since call numbers usually have to fit on the spine of the books, some libraries limit the length of the classification number for convenience.

Book Numbers

There are many types of book number. They include:

- a running number for each resource classed at the same number—for example:

625.1	625.1	625.1	625.2
1	2	3	1

  This is easy to apply, but does not arrange the resources in alphabetical order of author, and separates different editions of the same title.

- the first three (sometimes four) letters of the author's surname, or the title if there is no author—for example:

625.1	625.1	625.1	625.2
MAC	MAC	MAD	BAT

  This is also easy to apply, and arranges the resources in alphabetical order of surname or title, but results in some call numbers being identical.

- the first three (sometimes four) letters of the author's surname, or the title, followed by a number to make each call number unique—for example:

625.1	625.1	625.1	625.2
MAC	MAC.1	MAD	BAT

  This arranges the resources in approximate alphabetical order of surname or title, but care needs to be taken not to duplicate book numbers when allocating them.

- a Cutter-Sanborn number (also called a Cutter number) taken from the *Cutter-Sanborn three-figure author table.* This table enables a library to have a unique call number for every item, while maintaining alphabetical arrangement by surname—for example:

625.1	625.1	625.1	625.2
M118	M135	M179	B329

This arranges the resources in alphabetical order of surname or title, but it requires use of the Cutter Table, and care needs to be taken to allocate book numbers correctly. Detailed instructions on how to create these numbers are included in the Cutter-Sanborn Table.

Book Numbers for Biographies

It is common for the book number for biographies to be taken from the subject of the biography, rather than the author. A second symbol is sometimes added to represent the author's surname.

Shelflisting

A shelflist is the record of the resources in a library. Items in the shelflist are arranged in the same order as the resources on the shelves.

Before automation, one card from each set of catalog cards was filed in the shelflist, which was accessible only to library staff. It was used:

- to guide classifiers as to the use of a particular number
- to check the most recent allocation of book numbers if the library used unique call numbers
- to show classifiers which numbers were used previously, to maintain consistency
- as an aid to collection development, to show the strengths, weaknesses and gaps in the collection
- as an inventory record, for stocktaking
- as a historical and statistical record of the collection
- as an insurance record
- to provide subject bibliographies for reference staff.

Almost all these functions can be performed by the automated catalog, and increasingly libraries do not maintain a separate shelflist:

- The need for a unique call number is reduced, since in most automated systems the circulation records are controlled by a separate barcode.
- Stocktaking (where it still occurs) is done by reading the barcodes on the items with a wand, and using the automated system to compare this information with its database.
- Classification numbers can be checked direct from the catalog.
- Subject bibliographies can be produced by the system.
- In an automated system, each item has only one record with several access points, compared with the several cards for each item in a card catalog. Therefore the catalog is an accurate historical and statistical record and inventory, provided that it is backed up regularly and a backup copy is stored off-site.

Where automated libraries do have a separate shelflist, consideration must be given to its usefulness, compared with the cost of maintaining it.

REVISION QUIZ 3.3

Use the following questions to revise your understanding of the principles of classifying with DDC. You do not need to write down the answers.

1. How much of a resource do you need to examine to determine its subject?

2. Why is it important to decide the discipline?

3. Describe the difference between broad and close classification. Give an example.

4. What is citation order? What is preference order? Are they the same?

5. What does a call number consist of, and what is its purpose?

6. List 3 functions of a traditional shelflist that can be performed by an online catalog.

CHAPTER FOUR
Components of the Dewey Decimal Classification

Introduction
Volume 1 of DDC contains an introduction that explains the principles, structure and operation of the Classification. Much of it can be read immediately. Leave the sections you find too technical until you have begun to use DDC, and then try again – you will find it all makes sense once you have developed an understanding of the scheme.

Glossary
Volume 1 also contains a glossary of technical terms.

Overview – The Summaries

Ten Main Classes
Dewey Decimal Classification is designed to encompass all knowledge, dividing it into ten very broad classes – one for general works and nine for subject disciplines. This is called the First Summary. You may find it useful to memorize it, since knowing the overall structure will help you use the scheme more effectively.

The Summaries can be found at the front of Volume 2.

The First Summary lists the ten classes, as shown below:

First Summary
The Ten Main Classes

000 Computer science, information & general works

100 Philosophy & psychology

200 Religion

300 Social sciences

400 Language

500 Science

600 Technology

700 Arts & recreation

800 Literature

900 History & geography

Once you have identified the subject of an item, you need to place it in one or other of these ten classes. For example,

subject	discipline	class
logic	philosophy	100
Buddhism	religion	200
economics	social sciences	300
Latin grammar	language	400
chemistry	natural science	500
engineering	technology	600
sculpture	the arts	700
poetry	literature	800
history of Indonesia	history	900

 EXERCISE 4.1

Write the class number for each of the following:

1.   My book of opera   _____

2.   A child's Bible   _____

3.   Three Irish plays   _____

4.   World Book encyclopedia   _____

5.   Teach yourself Vietnamese   _____

6.   The psychology of violence   _____

7.   Russian rockets   _____

8.   Physics for beginners   _____

9.   Road atlas of New Zealand   _____

10. Employment of aged persons   _____

11. Multicultural education   _____

12. Encyclopaedia of Papua New Guinea   _____

13. How to draw cartoons   _____

14. Introductory philosophy   _____

15. Agricultural pest control   _____

The Hundred Divisions

Each class is divided into ten divisions. Each division represents a part of the discipline. This is the second summary.

Second Summary
The Hundred Divisions

000	Computer science, knowledge & systems	500	Science
010	Bibliographies	510	Mathematics
020	Library & information sciences	520	Astronomy
030	Encyclopedias & books of facts	530	Physics
040	[Unassigned]	540	Chemistry
050	Magazines, journals & serials	550	Earth sciences & geology
060	Associations, organizations & museums	560	Fossils & prehistoric life
070	News media, journalism & publishing	570	Biology
080	Quotations	580	Plants (Botany)
090	Manuscripts & rare books	590	Animals (Zoology)
100	Philosophy	600	Technology
110	Metaphysics	610	Medicine & health
120	Epistemology	620	Engineering
130	Parapsychology & occultism	630	Agriculture
140	Philosophical schools of thought	640	Home & family management
150	Psychology	650	Management & public relations
160	Philosophical logic	660	Chemical engineering
170	Ethics	670	Manufacturing
180	Ancient, medieval & eastern philosophy	680	Manufacture for specific uses
190	Modern western philosophy	690	Construction of buildings
200	Religion	700	Arts
210	Philosophy & theory of religion	710	Area planning & landscape architecture
220	The Bible	720	Architecture
230	Christianity	730	Sculpture, ceramics & metalwork
240	Christian practice & observance	740	Graphic arts & decorative arts
250	Christian pastoral practice & religious orders	750	Painting
260	Christian organization, social work & worship	760	Printmaking & prints
270	History of Christianity	770	Photography, computer art, film, video
280	Christian denominations	780	Music
290	Other religions	790	Sports, games & entertainment
300	Social sciences, sociology & anthropology	800	Literature, rhetoric & criticism
310	Statistics	810	American literature in English
320	Political science	820	English & Old English literatures
330	Economics	830	German & related literatures
340	Law	840	French & related literatures
350	Public administration & military science	850	Italian, Romanian & related literatures
360	Social problems & social services	860	Spanish, Portuguese & Galician literatures
370	Education	870	Latin & Italic literatures
380	Commerce, communications & transport	880	Classical & modern Greek literatures
390	Customs, etiquette & folklore	890	Other literatures
400	Language	900	History
410	Linguistics	910	Geography & travel
420	English & Old English languages	920	Biography & genealogy
430	German & related languages	930	History of ancient world (to ca. 499)
440	French & related languages	940	History of Europe
450	Italian, Romanian & related languages	950	History of Asia
460	Spanish, Portuguese, Galician	960	History of Africa
470	Latin & Italic languages	970	History of North America
480	Classical & modern Greek languages	980	History of South America
490	Other languages	990	History of other areas

EXERCISE 4.2

Using the second summary, write down the number of the division in which each of the following topics belongs. First decide the class, then the division.

1. Audiovisual materials in libraries   _____

2. Japanese printmaking   _____

3. Growing wheat for export   _____

4. Twentieth century architecture   _____

5. A concise history of Chile   _____

6. The nursing handbook   _____

7. Palaeontological studies   _____

8. Encouraging women into politics   _____

9. A historical atlas of ancient Egypt   _____

10. Carnivorous plants   _____

11. The Methodist Church in the Pacific   _____

12. Abortion   _____

13. The planet Mars   _____

14. How to play hockey   _____

15. Learn Polish : an audiovisual approach   _____

16. The Oxford English dictionary   _____

17. Caring for rare books   _____

18. Child psychology   _____

19. The legal handbook   _____

20. Jewish folk tales   _____

The Thousand Sections

Each division is divided into ten sections. Each section is a whole number that represents a topic. This is the third summary.

It is useful to spend some time looking through the third summary, since it provides a more detailed overview of the content of the Classification scheme. However, in order to locate classification numbers, you need to refer to the schedules, usually via the Relative Index.

Here is part of the third summary:

Third Summary
The Thousand Sections

000	Computer science, information & general works	050	General serial publications
001	Knowledge	051	Serials in American English
002	The book	052	Serials in English
003	Systems	053	Serials in other Germanic languages
004	Computer science	054	Serials in French, Occitan & Catalan
005	Computer programming, programs & data	055	In Italian, Romanian & related languages
006	Special computer methods	056	Serials in Spanish, Portuguese & Galician
007	[Unassigned]	057	Serials in Slavic languages
008	[Unassigned]	058	Serials in Scandinavian languages
009	[Unassigned]	059	Serials in other languages
010	Bibliography	060	General organizations & museum science
011	Bibliographies & catalogs	061	Organizations in North America
012	Bibliographies & catalogs of individuals	062	Organizations in British Isles; in England
013	[Unassigned]	063	Organizations in Germany; in central Europe
014	Of anonymous & pseudonymous works	064	Organizations in France & Monaco
015	Of works from specific places	065	In Italy, San Marino, Vatican City, Malta
016	Of works on specific subjects	066	In Spain, Andorra, Gibraltar, Portugal
017	General subject catalogs	067	Organizations in Russia; in eastern Europe
018	[Unassigned]	068	Organizations in other geographic areas
019	[Unassigned]	069	Museum science
020	Library & information sciences	070	News media, journalism & publishing
021	Library relationships	071	Newspapers in North America
022	Administration of physical plant	072	Newspapers in British Isles
023	Personnel management	073	Newspapers in Germany; in central Europe
024	[Unassigned]	074	Newspapers in France & Monaco
025	Library operations	075	In Italy, San Marino, Vatican City, Malta
026	Libraries for specific subjects	076	In Spain, Andorra, Gibraltar, Portugal
027	General libraries	077	Newspapers in Russia; in eastern Europe
028	Reading & use of other information media	078	Newspapers in Scandinavia
029	[Unassigned]	079	Newspapers in other geographic areas
030	General encyclopedic works	080	General collections
031	Encyclopedias in American English	081	Collections in American English
032	Encyclopedias in English	082	Collections in English
033	In other Germanic languages	083	Collections in other Germanic languages
034	Encyclopedias in French, Occitan & Catalan	084	Collections in French, Occitan & Catalan
035	In Italian, Romanian & related languages	085	In Italian, Romanian & related languages
036	Encyclopedias in Spanish, Portuguese & Galician	086	Collections in Spanish, Portuguese & Galician
037	Encyclopedias in Slavic languages	087	Collections in Slavic languages
038	Encyclopedias in Scandinavian languages	088	Collections in Scandinavian languages
039	Encyclopedias in other languages	089	Collections in other languages
040	[Unassigned]	090	Manuscripts & rare books
041	[Unassigned]	091	Manuscripts
042	[Unassigned]	092	Block books
043	[Unassigned]	093	Incunabula
044	[Unassigned]	094	Printed books
045	[Unassigned]	095	Books notable for bindings
046	[Unassigned]	096	Books notable for illustrations
047	[Unassigned]	097	Books notable for ownership or origin
048	[Unassigned]	098	Prohibited works, forgeries & hoaxes
049	[Unassigned]	099	Books notable for format

EXERCISE 4.3

Using the third summary, decide the section in which each of the following topics belongs. First decide the class, then the division, then look for the section:

1. Developing educational curricula   _____

2. Harrap's new German grammar   _____

3. The plays of William Shakespeare   _____

4. Electricity   _____

5. Let's visit Kenya   _____

6. The philosophy of Socrates   _____

7. South-East Asian cooking   _____

8. What bird is that?   _____

9. Journalism in the new Russia   _____

10. Steam trains for enthusiasts   _____

11. Islam   _____

12. Introduction to trout fishing   _____

The Schedules

Introduction

The schedules provide a systematic breakdown of the main classes, their divisions and their sections. More than 40,000 numbers are listed, in a straight numerical sequence from 000 to 999. In addition, numbers can be made by using the number-building features of DDC. These are treated in Chapters 7–12 of this workbook.

The principle of hierarchy that governs the scheme means:

broad numbers – broad subjects		specific numbers – specific subjects	
e.g., 500	science	551.6365	long-range weather forecasting
780	music	787.8719366	techniques for playing the guitar left-handed

In general, the longer the DDC number, the more specific is the subject it represents.

Hierarchy in the Schedules

In the overall hierarchy of DDC the 10 classes are divided into 100 divisions and 1000 sections. Each division is a specific aspect of its main class, and (almost) every section is a specific aspect of the division in which it is found.

 For example,

within	900	History and geography
we find	930	History of ancient world

within	930	History of ancient world
we find	938	Greece (history of ancient)

This principle extends into the schedules.

 For example,

900	History and geography
930	History of ancient world to ca. 499
938	Greece to 323 (history of)
938.03	Persian Wars, 500–479 B.C. (part of the history of Greece to 323)

Here each topic within **900 – History and geography** is a more specific aspect of the subject above it.

In this example, 938.03 is described as subordinate to 938;   938 is superordinate to 938.03.

 EXERCISE 4.4

Using the above example, complete the following:

1.   900 is superordinate to _____ .

2.   930 is _____ to 900.

3.   _____ is subordinate to 938.

Layout of the Hierarchical Structure

The layout of the schedules shows the hierarchy both by type size and by indentation.

Here is the same hierarchy again as printed in the schedules, showing clearly the subordination of the more specific numbers:

900 History and geography
930   History of ancient world to ca. 499
938   Greece to 323
938.03   Persian Wars, 500–479 B.C.

As you read the subordinate numbers, remember to include the superordinate headings above, since they are not always repeated for each more specific topic.

The Tables

DDC contains six auxiliary tables. They are used to build more specific numbers than are listed in the schedules.

For example, for almost every topic, it may be necessary to add a geographic aspect—e.g., there may be resources on trade unionism in most places in the world. So that the schedules do not have to list each topic for every place, the scheme allows a constant number for a place to be added to the number for almost any topic. The numbers for geographic places are found in an auxiliary table, Table 2.

In the same way, there are dictionaries or encyclopedias of many subjects. DDC allows the classifier to construct a specific number for a dictionary of religion by adding to the schedule number for religion a number that represents dictionaries from an auxiliary table, Table 1.

The auxiliary tables are:
    Table 1   Standard subdivisions
    Table 2   Geographic areas, historical periods, biography
    Table 3   Subdivisions for the arts, for individual literatures, for specific literary forms
    Table 4   Subdivisions of individual languages and language families
    Table 5   Ethnic and national groups
    Table 6   Languages

Numbers in the auxiliary tables are intended to be used only with numbers from the schedules, never alone. They are always quoted as T1—, T2—, T3— etc., to show that they are added to an existing classification number.

The auxiliary tables follow the Introduction in Volume 1. Numbers can only be added from the tables by following particular rules. The auxiliary tables are treated in Chapters 7–11 of this workbook.

The Manual

The Manual gives advice about how to classify difficult topics, especially where it may be hard to choose between two possible numbers.

For example, 'probabilities in games of chance' appear in different places in the classification scheme – in the 790s for recreational activities, and the 519s for mathematical probabilities. The relevant parts of the Schedules, 795.015192 and 519.27, refer to the Manual – *See Manual at 795.015192 vs. 519.27*. The Manual at 795.015192 *vs.* 519.27 explains the specific uses of each number, and concludes 'If in doubt, prefer 795.015192.'

It is very useful to consult the Manual when assistance or more information is needed. The Manual follows the Introduction in Volume 1.

The Relative Index

The Relative Index relates subjects to the disciplines of which they are part. The subjects are arranged alphabetically, showing the disciplines where they are treated.

 For example,

Computers	004
access control	005.8
management	658.478
elementary education	374.34
engineering	621.39
instructional use	371.334
adult level	374.26
primary level	372.133 4
law	343.099 9
maintenance	004.028 8
music	780.285
musical instruments	786.76
repair	004.028 8
social effects	303.483 4
theft of	345.026 280 04
law	364.162 800 4

The first number given (004) is the interdisciplinary number for a resource on computers. Listed below the heading are alternative numbers for computers, depending on the discipline where they belong, or the aspect of the subject being emphasized.

It is important to decide on the class before consulting the Relative Index. Then the class will help locate the best number for the subject.

    For example,

The electronic performance of computers belongs in Technology (600s).

Look at the index entry for computers. There are only two numbers in the 600s – one in the 620s (Engineering) and one in the 650s (Management). So the number 621.39 seems the best choice.

Terms in the Relative Index
The following are included in the Relative Index:
*   terms found in the headings and notes of the schedules
*   synonyms
*   selected terms in common use
*   names of countries, their states and provinces
*   names of counties in the USA
*   names of capital cities and other important municipalities
*   names of certain important geographical features—e.g., Pacific Ocean
*   heads of state used to identify historical periods—e.g., Louis XIV
*   founders of religion—e.g., Muhammad
*   initiators of schools of thought—e.g., Adam Smith.

The following are <u>not</u> included in the Relative Index:
*   phrases beginning with the adjectival form of languages and countries—e.g., American short stories, French cooking
*   phrases containing general concepts represented by standard subdivisions such as education, statistics, laboratories and management—e.g., art education, educational statistics.

The Relative Index is found in Volume 4.

REVISION QUIZ 4.5

Use the following questions to revise your understanding of the components of DDC. You do not need to write down the answers.

1. What is the purpose of the First, Second and Third Summaries in the Dewey Decimal Classification? When would you use them?

2. What is the importance of disciplines in the Dewey Decimal Classification?

3. What is hierarchy in DDC and why is it important?

4. In the hierarchy
   150   Psychology
   155   Differential and developmental psychology
   155.4 Child psychology
   is 155 superordinate to or subordinate to 155.4? What does this mean?

5. If a DDC number is very long, is it more likely to be a specific number or a broad number? Why?

6. What is the role of the auxiliary tables?

7. Does the index contain all the subjects listed in the Schedules?

8. In this excerpt from the Relative Index, what is the interdisciplinary number for helicopters?
   Helicopters   387.733 52
       engineering   629.133 352
       military engineering   623.746 047
       piloting   629.132 525 2
       transportation services   387.733 52

9. Where would you look for a comparison of the use of 550 (Earth sciences) and 910 (Geography and travel)?

10. Where in DDC will you find a definition of the rule of three? What is it?

CHAPTER FIVE
Finding a Number in the Schedules

Introduction

To classify a resource, first determine the subject, then the discipline to which the subject belongs.

It is also important to consider the nature of the collection and its users, and whether there are any library policies (e.g., location of particular items, level of specificity, maximum number of digits) that may affect the classification.

Specific Aspects of a Subject

As well as a whole subject being more or less specific, aspects or facets of a subject can be more or less important.

 For example, to classify the topic 'Breeding horses in Spain in the 1970s', you must identify the main subject and each of the aspects of the subject.

Main subject:	Breeding horses
Secondary aspect:	in Spain
Secondary aspect:	in the 1970s.

Some classification numbers will allow you to include both secondary aspects of the subject and others will not. Sometimes, you will have to decide which of the secondary aspects is more important. Sometimes the citation or preference order makes this decision.

 EXERCISE 5.1

For the following subjects, identify the main subject, and as many secondary aspects of the subject (in any order) as you think there are.

1. An illustrated history of 15th century Japan

    Main subject: _____

    Secondary aspect: _____

    Secondary aspect: _____

2. A dictionary of terms for motorists

    Main subject: _____

    Secondary aspect: _____

3.   The history of glass-blowing in Venice in the Middle Ages

Main subject: _____

Secondary aspect: _____

Secondary aspect: _____

Secondary aspect: _____

Begin with the Class

Since the classes govern the overall structure, once you have decided what the resource is about, determine the class in which the main subject belongs.

Next, identify all the secondary aspects of the resource, and then the importance of each of these aspects.

   For example,

Censorship in Iran : an encyclopedia
Main subject: Censorship
Discipline (class):   Social sciences (300)
Secondary aspects: Iran
                        Encyclopedia
Order of importance: 1 – Censorship
                        2 – Iran
                        3 – Encyclopedia

 ## Looking for DDC Numbers – A Summary

1.   Determine:
     i.   subject
     ii.   discipline (class)
     iii. significant parts of the subject
     iv.   significant order of the parts.

2.   Look up the subject in the index, choosing the number that corresponds to the discipline.

3.   Check the number in the schedules to ensure that
    i.   it is correct
    ii.   it is at the required level of specificity.

 Never classify directly from the index. Always check the schedules.

Searching the Relative Index

Once you have decided what the resource is about, choose the most specific description of the subject. Always search the index first for the most specific term. If the term is not found, try a broader term.

In the Relative Index, terms are arranged alphabetically, word by word. Terms are indented below the main heading. The DDC numbers are spaced at every third number after the decimal point; this is only for convenience of reading.

See also references are used for synonyms, and for references to broader and related terms.

 EXERCISE 5.2

Assign DDC numbers to each of the following subjects.
    i.   *Decide what the subject is*
    ii.   *Decide which class it belongs to*
    iii.   *Look up the index – look for as specific a topic as possible*
    iv.   *Check the number in the schedules.*

1.   Keyword indexing: an introduction to KWIC and KWOC

    Class   _____   Specific term(s)   _____

    DDC number   _____

2.   Laws relating to the disposal of human remains

    Class   _____   Specific term(s)   _____

    DDC number   _____

3.   Home care nursing

Class _____   Specific term(s) _____

DDC number _____

4.   Homosexuality – right or wrong?

Class _____   Specific term(s) _____

DDC number _____

5.   The 12 tribes of Ancient Israel

Class _____   Specific term(s) _____

DDC number _____

6.   Build your house with adobe bricks

Class _____   Specific term(s) _____

DDC number _____

7.   Blood banks – a public service

Class _____   Specific term(s) _____

DDC number _____

8.   God in Islam

Class _____   Specific term(s) _____

DDC number _____

9.   How volcanoes are formed

Class _____   Specific term(s) _____

DDC number _____

10. Family counselling

    Class   _____ Specific term(s)   _____

    DDC number   _____

11. The psychology of perception

    Class   _____ Specific term(s)   _____

    DDC number   _____

12. Ancient Chinese philosophy

    Class   _____ Specific term(s)   _____

    DDC number   _____

13. Hazardous toys

    Class   _____ Specific term(s)   _____

    DDC number   _____

14. Architecture of school buildings

    Class   _____ Specific term(s)   _____

    DDC number   _____

15. The causes of World War II

    Class   _____ Specific term(s)   _____

    DDC number   _____

CHAPTER SIX
Organization of the Schedules

Reading the Schedules

Reading the full number and its complete heading depends on understanding the principle of hierarchy.

Here is an extract from the schedules:

302	*Social sciences*

    .2   **Communication**

  .2223   Symbols

To read the whole number, include the number at the top of the page, since most of the entries only show the decimal portion.
So,
    .2223   Symbols
is not the whole number. Find the superordinate (whole) number **302** at the top of this page, to read the number as 302.2223.

Similarly, the heading
    .2223   Symbols
is not clear, until you read back up the hierarchy to the heading above:
    .2   **Communication**

So, 302.2223 means Symbols of communication.

 EXERCISE 6.1

DDC numbers are hierarchical. Here is an example of a number and its hierarchy:

    796.8309 – BMX racing

        700   The arts
        790   Recreational and performing arts
        796   Athletic and outdoor sports and games
        796.6   Cycling and related activities
        796.62   Bicycle racing
        796.622   BMX (Bicycle motocross)

Break down these numbers in the same way, showing each step of the hierarchy on a separate line. After breaking down the number, reconstruct the topic and write it next to the complete number. Include enough detail from your reconstruction to identify the specific topic of the number.

1.   345.072

2.   659.143

3.   375.001

4.   599.972

5.   910.452

Interpreting the Schedules

Here is another extract. Open Volume 2 at this section of the schedules, and study it alongside the explanations below:

300 Social sciences

Class here behavioral studies, social studies	This is a **class-here** note, that tells us what to use the number for
Class a specific behavioral science with the science, e.g., psychology 150 ...	This is a **class-elsewhere** note, that refers us to a different number
For language, see 400; for history, see 900	These are **see references** that direct us to other locations for specific parts of the subject
See Manual at 300 vs. 600; also at 300–330 ...	This **see-Manual** note directs us to more detailed explanations in the Manual

SUMMARY

300.1–.9	**Standard subdivisions**	The many **summaries** of the coverage of a division or a number may help you find your way around
301	**Sociology and anthropology**	
302	**Social interaction**	
303	**Social processes**	
304	**Factors affecting social behavior**	
305	**Groups of people**	
306	**Culture and institutions**	
307	**Communities**	
...		

301   Sociology and anthropology
                ...

[.019]	Psychological principles Do not use; class in 302	**Square brackets** are used when numbers are not to be used, because the number is not assigned, or has been relocated or discontinued

Options

Parentheses are used for optional numbers that may suit individual libraries, but are not part of the standard notation.

 For example, DDC recognizes that Christianity is not the main religion of many users of the Classification. So, at 290, it provides some options:

(Options: To give preferred treatment or shorter numbers to a specific religion, use one of the following:

Option A: ...,
Option B: class in 210, and add to base number 21 the numbers following the base number for that religion in 292–299, e.g., Hinduism 210, Mahabharata 219.23. ...)

A few other optional numbers are also included—e.g.,

(372.243)   Upper level of primary education
              (Optional number; prefer 373.236)

Centered Entries

Many headings refer to a span of numbers, rather than a single number. In these cases, the heading is printed in the center of the page, and is marked by the symbol > in the number column.

 For example,

> **930–990 History of specific continents, countries, localities; extraterrestrial worlds**

All instructions under this heading apply to all numbers in the range 930–990. This saves having to provide the same information separately for each number.

Other Notes

There are other notes in the schedules, most of which are self-explanatory.

It is very important to read the relevant section of the schedule, including checking the hierarchy, and reading all the notes that apply to your number, as well as the superordinate numbers in the appropriate part of the hierarchy.

For example, when deciding on the number '635.9312 – Annuals', it is useful to read the notes at 635.9. Also read the Manual entry at 635.9 *vs.* 582.1, that is referred to under '635.9 Flowers and ornamental plants'.

EXERCISE 6.2

Find an example of each of these in the schedules. If you are not sure what a term means, check the glossary in Volume 1 of DDC or at the back of this book.

1. A heading

2. A summary

3. A centered entry

4. A subordinate number

5. A relocated topic

6. A class-elsewhere note

7. A see also reference

8. A see reference

9. A scope note

10. An option

EXERCISE 6.3

Which is the correct number in each of the following groups?
  i. Find each number in the schedules and identify the topic it represents
  ii. Choose the number that most closely represents the subject given

1. Sodium vapour lighting in public areas

   621.3276

   621.324

   628.95

2. Decorative horn carving

   788.94

   681.8

   736.6

3. Gold in folk-lore

    398.3

    398.365

    549.23

    739.22

    553.41

4. Victims of crime

    364.44

    362.88

    363.23

    365.46

5. Household heating

    665.5384

    621.4025

    644.1

6. Prevention of heart disease

    616.12

    617.412

    641.56311

    614.5912

EXERCISE 6.4

Find the following DDC numbers using the index and the schedules:

1. The history of the Punic wars   _____

2. An introduction to photochemistry   _____

3. Big game hunting   _____

4. How valleys are formed   _____

5. The ouija board in spiritualism   _____

6. The identification of waterbirds   _____

7. How to read maps   _____

8. The Lutheran Church in America   _____

9. New ideas in tax reform   _____

10. Unemployment resulting from technological change   _____

11. Cycle racing   _____

12. Behaviour of people in disasters   _____

13. Electricity from the wind   _____

14. Cleaning clothes at home   _____

15. Sculpture in wax and wood   _____

EXERCISE 6.5

Find the following DDC numbers using the index and the schedules:

1. Ethiopia under Italian rule _____

2. Drawing and preparing maps _____

3. Social responsibility of executive management _____

4. Talismans in witchcraft _____

5. Rules of Parliament _____

6. Detergent technology _____

7. Military intelligence _____

8. Ultrasonic vibrations _____

9. Design of roadworks _____

10. Sculpture in the twentieth century _____

11. Plant diseases _____

12. Speed drills for typing _____

13. The ethics of government _____

14. Music for the guitar _____

15. Discipline in the classroom _____

16. Zodiac: an astrological guide _____

17. Making trousers commercially _____

18. Looking after hawks and falcons _____

EXERCISE 6.6

Find the following DDC numbers using the index and the schedules:

1. A general introduction to the violin, cello and other
    bowed string instruments   _____

    2. Design and construction of clocks   _____

    3. Cookery in restaurants   _____

    4. How to code computer programs   _____

    5. The use of radio in adult education   _____

    6. Evolution of microbes   _____

    7. Growing carrots in the home garden   _____

    8. Techniques for indoor photography   _____

    9. Eighteenth century sculpture   _____

    10. Manufacture of paper   _____

    11. Triplets, quads and more: an obstetric guide   _____

    12. The Panama Canal: modern aid to transportation   _____

    13. The physics of auroras   _____

    14. Flying fishes and seahorses: odd marine creatures   _____

    15. A guide to cooking with pressure cookers   _____

CHAPTER SEVEN
Number-Building—Table 1: Standard Subdivisions

Introduction
DDC began as an enumerative classification scheme. That is, all the numbers were listed, and the classifier simply looked them up. Over time, the scheme has provided for more numbers to be constructed (synthesized) by adding to a number in the schedules.

Numbers can be built by adding to a base number
- from a table
- from another part of the schedule.

Chapters 7–11 deal with the auxiliary tables. Adding from another part of the schedules is covered in Chapter 12.

The Auxiliary Tables
The auxiliary tables in DDC are intended to be used only with numbers from the schedules, never alone. They are always quoted as T1—, T2—, T3— etc., to show that they are added to an existing classification number. There are six auxiliary tables:

Table 1	Standard subdivisions
Table 2	Geographic areas, historical periods, biography
Table 3	Subdivisions for the arts, individual literatures, for specific literary forms
Table 4	Subdivisions of individual languages and language families
Table 5	Ethnic and national groups
Table 6	Languages

With the exception of the standard subdivisions, they are only to be added to a classification number when special instructions appear at that number.

Unless special instructions are given, only one number from an auxiliary table can be added to a classification number. If more than one applies to a resource, there is a table of preference at the beginning of Table 1 (on page 180 of volume 1), and the classifier must choose the number that appears first in that table.

Table 1 – Standard Subdivisions
In non-fiction materials, there are some regular patterns of treatment. For example, in a subject such as Psychology, there are resources that deal with:

Philosophy and theory of psychology
Research in psychology
History of psychology
Psychology as practiced in different parts of the world

In the same way, a subject may appear in a number of recognized forms—e.g.,

Serial	Illustrated
Directory	Dictionary
Tables or statistics	Encyclopedia

In DDC, these regularly-recurring forms or treatments of a subject are recognized as 'standard' methods. This allows a resource to be classified at its main subject, and added to by using numbers from Table 1.

No special instructions from the schedules are needed to add standard subdivisions. They can be added freely, when needed, to any classification number, although only one is added for any one resource.

Useful standard subdivisions include:

-01   Philosophy and theory
-022 Illustrations, models, miniatures
-025 Directories of persons and organizations
-03   Dictionaries, encyclopedias, concordances
-05   Serial publications
-06   Organizations and management
-07   Education, research, related topics
-08   Groups of people
-09   History, geographic treatment, biography

The standard subdivision -09 is sometimes combined with numbers from Table 2, so that the geographic treatment can be linked to a specific country or location.

 For example,

Number from schedules	364	Criminology
+ standard subdivision	-09	Geographical treatment
+ number from Table 2	-714	Quebec
=	**364.097 14**	**Criminology in Quebec**

Purposes of Standard Subdivisions

Standard subdivisions are used:

* to make a classification number more specific
* to distinguish between different ways of treating the subject
* to describe how an item is treated, so that items dealing with a 'big' subject can be grouped together on the shelves.

 Brown   Smith

Theory of banking	Banking theory
332.101	332.101

As standard subdivisions begin with –0, DDC ensures that these 'standard' treatments of the subject can be shelved in their groups before the subject is further subdivided in the tables.

Brown	Jones	Adams	Carter
Theory of	History of	Commercial	Theory of
banking	banking	banks	commercial banks
332.101	332.109	332.12	332.120 1

If the schedules are already full at the –0 number, there are special directions on how to apply standard subdivisions at those numbers. Usually –001, –002, –003, etc. are used to keep the standard subdivisions at the beginning of the number for the topic.

 ## Principles for Applying Standard Subdivisions

1. They must never be used alone, but only with a number from the schedules. This is why they are always quoted as T1–01, –03 etc. The dash is not used in the combined number; it simply shows that the number is incomplete.

2. The digits in the standard subdivisions may be applied to any base number. If the base number is less than 3 digits, combine it with the standard subdivisions number, and add the decimal point where necessary.

Base number for technology	6 +
Trademarks & service marks	–0275
Trademarks & service marks of products =	602.75

3. Do not add one standard subdivision to another, unless there are specific instructions to do so.

When Not to Use the Standard Subdivisions
Although standard subdivisions are applicable throughout the schedules, under some circumstances they should not be used:
* When the number is already built into the schedules (e.g., 501, 502, 503). Always check the classification number to see if this is the case. Do not try to add standard subdivisions to a number found in the index.

* When they would be redundant (i.e., if the base number already means safety measures, it would be unnecessary to add –0289 – safety measures).

* When there is an instruction not to use the standard subdivisions.

* When the subject of the resource is more specific than the classification number. For example, a resource on Black widow spiders has to be classified at 595.44–Spiders, because there is no number that is more specific. In this case, don't add a standard subdivision. Many kinds of spiders will have to be grouped at this number, and in future editions of DDC new numbers may be developed to separate them. This space to add more specific numbers is called 'standing room'. Since any addition to the number now may conflict with a future expansion of the number, do not build further.

- When there is an 'including' note at a number. Including notes identify topics that are in 'standing room' and like the example above, standard subdivisions cannot be added to them, nor are any other number-building techniques allowed.

 For example, the number for military models and miniatures is 745.592 82, with a note saying '*including toy soldiers*'. It is possible to classify a magazine about all sorts of military models at 745.592 820 5 (using the standard subdivision –05 for serial publications), but a magazine specifically about toy soldiers can only be classified at 745.592 82.

How to Add from Table 1

1. *Identify the subject proper,* and then the element/s represented by standard subdivision(s)
2. *Classify the subject proper* – using the Relative Index and checking in the schedules
3. *Find the notation you need for the standard subdivision* – either using the Relative Index or directly from Table 1
4. *Check the schedules* to see whether there are any instructions about standard subdivisions
5. *Add the table number to the schedule number*
6. *Check the schedules again,* to ensure there is no conflict with a number or instruction.

 Encyclopedia of international law
Law of nations   341 +
   Encyclopedia   –03   =   341.03

The terminology of stars
   Stars   523.8 +
   Terminology   –014   =   523.801 4

Civil engineering as a profession
   Civil engineering   624 +
   As a profession   –023   =   624.023

Workbooks in algebra
   Algebra   512 +
   Workbooks   –076
   But 512 Algebra lists
        .001–.009   Standard subdivisions
   So
   Workbooks in algebra   =   512.007 6

EXERCISE 7.1

Construct DDC numbers for the following topics, using the Relative Index, the schedules and Table 1:

1.   Dictionary of child psychology

2.   Journal of manufacture of electronic toys

3.   The language of soccer

4.   Pony weekly magazine

5.   Teaching netball

6.   The philosophy of idealism

7.   The philosophy of social work

8.   Standards for lathes

9.   Dictionary of biochemistry

10. A history of child care

11. Systems of long-range weather forecasting

12. Sales catalogue of wedding dresses

13. Guidebook for a toy museum

14. The terrier encyclopaedia

15. Genetics research

16. Handicrafts for people with disabilities

EXERCISE 7.2

Look at the schedules and standard subdivisions in Table 1. Find the subject for each of the following numbers, and supply a suitable title. For example,

658.008 694 1 – Management skills for the unemployed

1. 796.352 05 _____

2.   370.3 _____

3. 371.003 _____

4. 372.03 _____

5. 375.000 3 _____

6. 629.132 300 5 _____

7. 181.005 _____

8. 336.002 85 _____

9. 621.388 007 2 _____

10. 730.74 _____

11. 300.724 _____

12. 512.005 _____

13. 512.705 _____

14. 338.430 007 2 _____

'Non-Standard' Addition of Standard Subdivisions

As you have seen in the last exercise, there are many places in the schedules where you cannot simply add the notation –01 etc. to the number in the schedule. These include

- main classes
- divisions
- some other numbers indicated in the schedules.

It is necessary to check the schedules, where most irregular usage is indicated by an instruction—e.g.,

> SUMMARY
> 540.1–.9   Standard subdivisions

or

> SUMMARY
> 335.001–335.009   Standard subdivisions

Also check the schedule for patterns. Where one standard subdivision is used in a particular way, the others follow the same pattern, unless otherwise instructed.

 For example,

500	**Natural sciences and mathematics**
501	**Philosophy and theory**
502	**Miscellany**

These are the standard subdivisions, so follow the pattern for all of them.

510	**Mathematics**
510.1	**Philosophy and theory**

The other standard subdivisions for Mathematics follow the same pattern, so Mathematics as a profession = 510.23

375	**Curricula**
.0001–.0009	Standard subdivisions

This pattern requires extra zeroes.

Use of –04 for Special Topics

Some numbers in the schedules make use of the standard subdivision –04, that is reserved for special topics.

 For example,

621	**Applied physics**
.04	Special topics of applied physics
.042	Energy engineering
.044	Plasma engineering

Facet Indicators

In the notation −09, 0 is called a facet indicator. That is, its purpose is to indicate that a facet is being added to the number. Facet indicators are sometimes shown as part of the base number. For example, in '634.82 Injuries, diseases and pests of grapes', 2 is added to the number 634.8, to introduce the special numbers for the facets of grape crops that follow.

EXERCISE 7.3

Assign DDC numbers to the following subjects, using the Relative Index, the schedules and Table 1.

1. Dictionary of library and information science   _____

2. Philosophy of library science   _____

3. Library and information science: a journal   _____

4. Dictionary of psychology   _____

5. Psychology: historical research   _____

6. Dictionary of ethics   _____

7. Ethics: a quarterly journal   _____

8. International architecture organisations   _____

9. Dictionary of architecture   _____

10. Study and teaching of chemical technology   _____

EXERCISE 7.4

Assign DDC numbers to the following subjects, using the Relative Index, the schedules and Table 1.

1. Popular engineering (quarterly journal)   _____

2. Agricultural pest control monthly   _____

3. Apparatus used in puppetry   _____

4. Correspondence courses in electronics   _____

5. Songs of the Middle Ages   _____

6. Encyclopedia of horses   _____

7. History of the social sciences   _____

8. Philosophy of Christianity   _____

9. Historical research into public administration   _____

10. Lives of ten great artists   _____

11. Theory of the solar system   _____

12. Research in oceanography   _____

13. Harness racing news (monthly journal)   _____

14. Theory of personnel management   _____

15. Book publishing trade catalogues   _____

16. Journal of the philosophy of socialism   _____
    (Hint: use the table of preference)

More than One Standard Subdivision

Some resources cover more than one aspect of their main subject, each of which could be represented by a standard subdivision. However, the rules prohibit use of more than one standard subdivision in most cases.

First consider whether one standard subdivision is much more important in the subject than the other(s).

 For example, in the subject 'research in Japanese photography', there are two possible standard subdivisions – research, and geographical treatment (Japan). The main subject is Japanese photography, so use the standard subdivision –09 to include the geographical aspect, and ignore the secondary aspect of research.

However, if the secondary aspects of the subject are of equal significance, refer to the table of preference at the beginning of Table 1. This shows which aspect of the subject to include.

 For example, a journal of economic geology research has the main topic economic geology, and two possible standard subdivisions, research and serials. In the table of preference, –072 (research) comes before –05 (serial publications), so the completed number will be

Economic geology	+	research		
553	+	–072	=	553.072

REVISION QUIZ 7.5

Use the following questions to revise your understanding of standard subdivisions. You do not need to write down the answers.

1. Why does DDC use standard subdivisions?

2. When can they be added?

3. How do you know that a number given in the Relative Index is a standard subdivision?

4. Are there situations where standard subdivisions should not be used? What are they?

5. What do the following standard subdivisions stand for?

    −01 _____

    −03 _____

    −05 _____

    −07 _____

    −09 _____

6. Why do standard subdivisions begin with −0?

7. Why do you need to check the schedules when constructing a number using a standard subdivision?

8. '335 Socialism and related systems' lists:
          .001–.009 Standard subdivisions
    What is the number for a dictionary of socialism?

9. What is the table of preference? When is it used?

10. Using the table of preference, which standard subdivision will you use for the topic 'Equipment and teaching in hydraulic engineering'?

CHAPTER EIGHT
Number-Building—Table 2: Geographic Areas, Historical Periods, Biography

Introduction

Table 2 is the largest table in the DDC. It consists mainly of place names, that are sometimes very specific—e.g., 'Birmingham and neighboring metropolitan boroughs of England', and sometimes more general—e.g., 'Thailand'. The more specific numbers tend to reflect the major English-speaking users of the classification scheme.

In addition to specific places, Table 2 provides for general geographic treatment by, for example, zone (e.g., tropics), type of vegetation (deserts), socioeconomic status (rural regions) and so on.

The historical periods listed in Table 1 are included in Table 2, so that they can be added in accordance with the instruction to 'Add ... from Table 2'. Similarly, −2 Biography is given here.

Geographic Treatment

A large number of subjects can be treated by place—e.g., football in the United States, Indian sculpture, cookery of Italy and so on.

Some parts of the schedules include the place as an integral part of the classification number.

 For example,

> **190** **Modern western and other non-eastern philosophy**
> 191 **United States and Canada**
> 192 **British Isles**
>
> and so on.

However, the geographic treatment of most subjects is represented by building a number using Table 2: Geographic areas, historical periods, biography (also called the Area table).

Table 2 (unlike Table 1) cannot be used without an instruction. The instruction always specifies the base number, and the section of the table that you are entitled to use, for example:

Add to base number 912 notation 3–9 from Table 2, e.g., ...

Study the summary at the beginning of Table 2.

−1 deals with places not limited by continent etc.—e.g., forests, oceans

−3 deals with the ancient world (although with the same overemphasis on European countries)

−4 to −9 cover the modern world, continent by continent. Within each continent, the notation divides into countries, then regions and so on.

Area numbers can be found either by following the division of the larger place, or by consulting the Relative Index.

Geography

The centered entry

> **913–919 Geography of and travel in specific continents, countries, localities; extraterrestrial worlds**

carries the instruction

Add to base number 91 notation 3–9 from Table 2, ...

That is, write down the base number 91, then check Table 2 for the particular place. Note that this instruction restricts the notation to 3–9. That is, you can construct a number for the geography of any specific place in the ancient or modern world, but not the geography of places in general, like forests (−152).

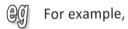 For example,

Geography of Stone County (Mississippi)				
Geography		91 +		
Stone County (Mississippi)			−762 162 =	917.621 62

Geography of the Great Barrier Reef				
Geography		91 +		
Great Barrier Reef			−943 =	919.43

Below the centered heading for 913–919, there is a table of other numbers to add, after you have made the geography number.

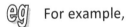 For example,

Travel in Stone County (Mississippi)		
Geography of Stone County (Mississippi)	917.621 62 +	
Travel	−04 =	917.621 620 4

An illustrated geography of the Great Barrier Reef		
Geography of the Great Barrier Reef	919.43 +	
Illustrations	−00222 =	919.430 022 2

EXERCISE 8.1

Assign DDC numbers to the following subjects:

1. The geography of Zimbabwe _____

2. A textbook of Papua New Guinea geography _____

3. The Amazon River: a geography _____

4. Geography of ancient Rhodes _____

5. A hotel guide to the French Riviera _____

6. The travellers' guide to Spain _____

7. Prehistoric geography of Carthage _____

8. An illustrated guide to the geography of ancient England _____

9. A gazetteer of Southern Africa _____

10. Bahrain on $100 a day _____

History

The centered entry

> **930–990   History of specific continents, countries, localities; of extraterrestrial worlds**

carries the instruction

Add to base number 9 notation 3–9 from Table 2, ...

That is, write down the base number 9, then check Table 2 for the particular place. Note that this instruction restricts the notation to 3–9. That is, you can construct a number for the history of any specific place in the ancient or modern world, but not the history of places in general, like forests (–152).

   For example,

History of Vietnam			
History	9 +		
Vietnam		–597	=	959.7

History of Mauritius			
History	9 +		
Mauritius		–6982	=	969.82

Remember that when you have added the table number to the base number, always put the decimal point after the third digit.

Periods of History

In the schedules, each country has its own period table, that must be used rather than the one in Table 1. These period tables apply to the country as a whole and to its subdivisions, such as states, provinces, cities etc.

   For example,

History of Vietnam under the French: 959.703
    History   9 +
    Vietnam   –597   =   959.7

Now check the schedules at 959.7:
    French period, 1883–1945   +03 = 959.703

History of Mauritius in the twentieth century: 969.820 2
    History   9 +
    Mauritius   –6982   =   969.82

Now check the schedules at 969.82:
    Period of British rule, ...
        Including 20th century   +02 = 969.820 2

EXERCISE 8.2

Assign DDC numbers to the following subjects:

1. A history of ancient Sparta   _____

2. A short history of the mountain regions of Bolivia   _____

3. Submarine warfare in the first World War   _____

4. The United States under President Ronald Reagan, 1981–1989   _____

5. A history of the Thirty Years War, 1618–1648   _____

6. The French Revolution   _____

7. The Russian Revolution   _____

8. History of the Persian Empire   _____

9. Norway in the 1950s: an outline history   _____

10. The encyclopedia of Zambian history   _____

Other Subjects

Many other subjects have instructions for adding from Table 2 to include geographic treatment in the complete classification number.

 For example,

372.9   History, geographic treatment, biography of primary education

carries the instruction at '.91–.99 Geographic treatment':

Add to base number 372.9 notation 1–9 from Table 2, ...

Elementary education in Brazil
Base number   372.9 +
Brazil   –81   =   372.981

EXERCISE 8.3

Assign DDC numbers to the following subjects:

1.   Geology of Quebec   _____

2.   Printmaking in Japan   _____

3.   General statistics of Hungary   _____

4.   Political conditions in the Irish Republic   _____

5.   Economic conditions in Algeria   _____

6.   Higher education in Vietnam   _____

7.   Libraries in New Zealand   _____

8.   The Roman Catholic Church in Paraguay   _____

9.   Constitutional law of ancient China   _____

10. Life expectancy in Burundi   _____

Adding From Table 2 Without Instructions

There are many subjects in the schedules that may need geographical treatment, but have no special instructions to add from Table 2.

However, special instructions are not needed to add from Table 1. So first add –09 from Table 1, then the area notation from Table 2.

 For example,

Boxing in Mexico
Boxing   796.83 +
Add –09 from Table 1   –09
Mexico (from Table 2)   –72   =   796.830 972

 EXERCISE 8.4

Assign DDC numbers to the following subjects:

1. Snowmobiling in Scotland

2. New Orleans brass bands

3. Design and construction of buildings in Nagasaki

4. Working mothers in ancient Rome

5. Family counselling in Sweden

EXERCISE 8.5

Look at the schedules and Tables 1 and 2. Find the subject for each of the following numbers, and supply a suitable title. For example,

324.249 650 75 – The Communist Party of Albania

1. 942.052 007 2 _____

2. 994.040 05 _____

3. 306.743 094 93 _____

4. 283.946 _____

5. 372.9593 _____

6. 996.11 _____

7. 359.009 611 _____

8. 759.949 2 _____

9. 026.340 025 766 38 _____

10. 994.230 609 22 _____

EXERCISE 8.6

Assign DDC numbers to the following subjects. They include numbers direct from the schedules, and numbers built by using Tables 1 and 2.

1. Raising pigs   _____

2. How to make soft toys   _____

3. Surfacing dirt roads   _____

4. Mobility of labour   _____

5. Problems providing food, clothing and shelter for those in need   _____

6. The encyclopedia of household pets   _____

7. Teaching drawing   _____

8. The theory of underwater photography   _____

9. The philosophy of evolution   _____

10. Correspondence course in mathematics   _____

11. Radio in the 1930s   _____

12. The sociology of slavery in the Roman Empire   _____

13. Death customs in ancient Britain   _____

14. Theatre in Botswana   _____

15. Air pollution controls in Mexico   _____

16. Political parties in Peru   _____

17. Alligators of the Florida Everglades   _____

18. Gold mining in the Kimberleys of Western Australia   _____

19. Firefighting in South Australia   _____

20. Firefighting in the Flinders Ranges of South Australia   _____

EXERCISE 8.7

Assign DDC numbers to the following subjects. They include numbers direct from the schedules, and numbers built by using Tables 1 and 2.

1.   Modern archaeology: techniques and equipment   _____

2.   The dictionary of place names   _____

3.   Maps of Irian Jaya   _____

4.   New South Wales during the Federation movement   _____

5.   Scotland in the 1960s   _____

6.   Ohio history quarterly   _____

7.   The diplomatic history of World War II   _____

8.   Exploration of Mars   _____

9.   Lake fishing   _____

10. Marine transportation across the Atlantic Ocean   _____

11. Baboons of the grasslands   _____

12. Wind systems in valleys   _____

13. Paintings in the 17th century   _____

14. Ancient Egypt during the Middle Kingdom   _____

15. The Thai Historical Association journal   _____

16. Life expectancy in Spain   _____

17. Modern British philosophy   _____

18. Customs of Easter Island   _____

19. Dictionary of building   _____

20. Experimental research in pharmaceutical chemistry   _____

CHAPTER NINE
Number-Building—Table 3: Subdivisions for the Arts, for Individual Literatures, for Specific Literary Forms

Introduction

Table 3 is used with numbers from the 800 class – Literature and rhetoric. (Rhetoric is the branch of knowledge that treats the rules or principles of effective composition, whether in prose or verse; the art that teaches oratory).

The 800s are used for works of the imagination; works of information should be classed with the subject.

Literature is restricted to:
- works of the imagination that are written in a particular form—e.g., poetry, fiction, drama
- criticism or description of such works
- history of a form (literary history) and biographies of authors.

There are 3 sub-tables:
Table 3A	works by or about individual authors
Table 3B	works by or about more than one author
Table 3C	only used when an extra aspect of the work has to be added.

Language

Literature is first treated according to the language in which it was originally written. The 800s are divided into:

800–809	Literature and rhetoric (in general)
810–819	American literature in English
820–829	English & Old English literatures
830–839	German & related literatures
840–849	French & related literatures
850–859	Italian, Romanian, & related literatures
860–869	Spanish, Portuguese, Galician literatures
870–879	Latin & Italic literatures
880–889	Classical Greek & related literatures
890–899	Literatures of other languages

Clearly this overemphasis on certain European literatures reflects the bias of American scholarship in Melvil Dewey's time. The allocation of so many literatures into 890–899 results in some very long numbers.

There is also bias in favor of the 'mother country' of the language, so that American and British literatures are well provided for, but Australian, Canadian, New Zealand, Indian, West Indian and South African literatures in English are not.

This fault cannot be rectified without restructuring the 800s. Options are provided in an attempt to accommodate particular needs. For example, one option is to use 810–819 or 820–829, and distinguish various literatures by the use of initial letters (e.g., Canada—C810, Australia—A820, New Zealand—NZ820).

While this option keeps the works of each literature together, it creates filing and shelving difficulties, especially when computers do the filing. Other options are described under 810–890.

Each library has its own policy for classifying literature that 'requires local emphasis'. Since practice varies, you should familiarize yourself with the policy and usage of one library you know well.

Form
The literary form of the work is considered next. Forms in Table 3 include:
- −1 Poetry
- −2 Drama
- −3 Fiction
- −4 Essays
- −5 Speeches
- −6 Letters
- −7 Humor and satire
- −8 Miscellaneous writings.

Some of these forms are further subdivided—e.g., Romantic fiction is a subdivision of Fiction. There is a preference table to look up when resources have more than one form—e.g., a play in verse.

Period
Each major literature is further divided into recognized time periods. These are listed in the schedules at the number for the individual literature.

Other Aspects
It is also possible for the DDC number to reflect particular aspects of a group of resources. Classification numbers can represent resources on a theme (e.g., Christmas), by particular people (e.g., children), or with a special feature (e.g., an experimental approach).

Literary Criticism

Literary criticism is classed with the literature being criticized. So discussion or criticism of a resource is at the same number as the resource itself (except optionally for Shakespeare and other very prolific authors). Criticism of several literatures is classed in 809.

Adaptations

An adaptation alters the form of a work or modifies its content in language, scope, or level of presentation so that it can no longer be considered a version of the original. It should then be classed as a work in its own right.

How to Add from Table 3

First decide whether the work is by one author or more than one author.

Table 3A – Works by or about One Author

1. *Determine the original language.* (This includes translations, which are classed with the original language)
    Use the schedules (810–890) to find the base number for the language
        e.g., English   82

    Note that numbers from Table 3 can only be added to a base number – identified by the words 'base number' or an asterisk (*) – or where there is an instruction to add from Table 3. If a literature is not identified in this way, do not add from Table 3. For example, Shan poetry is classed at 895.919 *not* 895.9191

2. *If there is a specific literary form*:
    Use Table 3A to find the number for the form
        e.g., poetry   −1
    Add it to the base number
        e.g., English poetry   82 + 1   =   821

    If there is no specific literary form:
    Go to the instructions under −8 in Table 3A

3. *If there is a specific period*:
    Use the schedules (810–890) to find the period table
        e.g., English poetry of the Victorian period   821 + 8 = 821.8

    Note that there are optional period tables for other English-language literatures – for Australia, Canada and so on.

EXERCISE 9.1

Find the base number for the following literatures:

1. American (in English)   _____

2. Dutch   _____

3. Swedish   _____

4. French   _____

5. Italian   _____

6. Catalan   _____

7. Portuguese   _____

8. Classical Greek   _____

9. Urdu   _____

10. Assamese   _____

11. Breton   _____

12. Slovenian   _____

13. Kota   _____

14. Korean   _____

15. Xhosa   _____

EXERCISE 9.2

Find a DDC number for the following, using the schedules and Table 3A:

1. Poetry by an American poet   _____

2. A drama in Dutch by one author   _____

3. A collection of a Swedish novelist   _____

4. Short stories in English translation by a French author   _____

5. Letters written by a high-ranking Italian lady   _____

6. Speeches in Catalan by a famous politician   _____

7. A Portuguese author's miscellaneous writings   _____

8. Classical Greek poetry by a medieval poet   _____

9. 20th century drama by an Urdu author   _____

10. A modern Assamese novel   _____

11. Letters by a 16th century Breton   _____

12. Speeches by a Slovenian citizen in 1920–1930   _____

13. Poems of a Kota woman   _____

14. Reminiscences of a Korean during the Yi period   _____

15. Xhosa fiction   _____

Table 3B – Works by or about More than One Author

1. *Determine the original language.* (This includes translations, which are classed with the original language)
    Use the schedules to find the base number for the language
    > e.g., Chinese   895.1

2. *If there is a specific literary form*:
    Use Table 3B to find the number for the form
    > e.g., drama   −2
    Add it to the base number
    > e.g., Chinese drama   895.1 + 2   =   895.12
    If there is no specific literary form:
    Go to the instructions under −01−09 in Table 3B

3.   *If the literary form can be specified further* (e.g., tragedy)
      Use Table 3B to find the more specific form
            e.g., tragedy   −20512
      Add it to the base number
            e.g., Chinese tragedy   895.1 + 20512   =   895.120 512

      If the literary form cannot be specified further, and if there is a specific period, go to step 4

4.   *If there is a specific period*:
      Use the schedules to find the period table
            e.g., Chinese drama of the Ming dynasty
                        895.12   +   46   =   895.124 6

EXERCISE 9.3

Find a DDC number for the following, using the schedules and Table 3A or 3B. Decide first whether the work is by one or more than one author:

1.   The Penguin book of Chinese verse   _____

2.   Fifteenth century English drama   _____

3.   French essays between the World Wars   _____

4.   A yearbook of Finnish literature   _____

5.   Essays of Umberto Eco translated from the Italian (late 20th century)   _____

6.   War and peace, a novel by Leo Tolstoy, translated from the Russian   _____

7.   Mother Courage and her children, by Berthold Brecht, a tragedy translated from German, written 1936–1939   _____

8.   Letters home: letters of Sylvia Plath, US poet, late 20th century   _____

9.   Famous Greek ballads of the nineteenth century   _____

10.   The Spanish love story   _____

Complex Numbers for Literature

It is possible to build extremely complex DDC numbers for literary works—for example:

An anthology of English limericks about cats	821.075 083 629 752
American television plays about death	812.025 083 548

However, for many libraries this level of close classification is not appropriate. Libraries need to consider how many resources they will have on these subjects, and weigh the advantages of specificity against the disadvantages of very long numbers – on spines, on OPAC screens, for users to write down, for library staff to shelve and so on.

Many libraries have policies about how specific their literature numbers are. For example, a library may decide that in the literature of a single language, only the form and time period will be reflected. Remember that classification is for the purpose of shelving similar resources together, and helping users to find the material they want. Extremely long numbers are likely to be useful only in very large literature collections, where users are interested in very specific aspects of the literary works.

Complex Number-Building : Tables 3B and 3C

For full use of Table 3B, read and follow the instructions given at the beginning of the table. There is also a detailed explanation, including flowcharts, in the Manual entry on Table 3.

Many sections of Table 3B refer to another section, where instructions are to be followed. Be especially careful whether they refer to **–1–8** or **–102–108**.

Remember only to add to any DDC number when there are instructions to add (other than standard subdivisions).

Table 3C—To Be Added Where Instructed

Table 3C enables many aspects of a literary work to be classified, including specific qualities of style (e.g., post-modernism), themes (e.g., seasons), subjects (e.g., religion), and persons (e.g., for and by children, Vietnamese).

This table can also be used with some base numbers in the 700s.

   For example,

Urban themes in the arts		700.421 732
	700.4	Special topics in the arts (schedules – base number)
	2	places (number following –3 in –32 in Table 3C)
	1732	urban regions (Table 2)

Films portraying the Bible		791.436 822
	791.436	Special aspects of films (schedules – base number)
	82	Religious themes (number following –3 in –382 in Table 3C)
	2	Bible (number following 2 in 220 Bible)

EXERCISE 9.4

Break down each step in the construction of the following numbers. You do not need to construct the numbers yourself.

   Example: Collections of contemporary English-language poetry about Lincolnshire
        821.914 080 324 253

82		*English language literature (schedules – base number)*
1		*poetry (table 3B)*
914		*later 20th century (schedules – English period table)*
0		*(as instructed at –11–19 in table 3B)*
80		*collections (table 3B)*
32		*about places (table 3C)*
4253		*Lincolnshire (table 2)*

1. A collection of poetry for children   821.008 092 82

2. An anthology of American poetry about animals   811.008 036 2

3. Poems by English women, Elizabethan to Victorian   821.008 092 87

4. An anthology of modern English drama   822.914 08

5. A book of contemporary Latin-American short stories   863.010 886 8

6. Best sellers by French teenagers   843.009 928 3

7. A critical study of Manx literature   891.640 9

8. Soviet literature of the 1980s : a decade of transition   891.709 004 4

9. The Virago book of ghost stories   823.087 33

10. The journal of Beatrix Potter from 1881–1897   828.803

11. The grotesque in the arts   700.415

12. Comedy films   791.436 17

Options for Australian, Canadian, New Zealand Literature

The 800 class devotes one division to American literature and one division to English literature. In countries where another literature in English (e.g., Australian, Canadian, New Zealand, Irish) is particularly important, a number of options are available.

An option for Australian literature is to use the numbers in '820–829 – English & Old English literatures', with **A** in front of them—e.g., A822 for Australian drama.

Use of initial letters for the English-language literatures of specific countries can be applied to other countries, for example India (In), New Zealand (NZ), Wales (W), Ireland (Ir) etc.

Other options are described under 810-890. Where one of the options is used for particular literatures, assign the optional period numbers provided in the schedules.

For Canadian literature in English, options include:
- using 810–818 for American literature and 819 for Canadian literature in English
- classifying Canadian literature in English with American literature in 810–818
- using C810–C818 for Canadian literature in English
- classifying Canadian literature in English with English literature in 820–828

A similar set of options is available for Canadian literature in French, the literature of American countries in Spanish or Portuguese, and for other literatures requiring local emphasis.

 EXERCISE 9.5

Classify the following Australian and New Zealand literary resources using the option of beginning the number with A or NZ.
Classify the Canadian resources using any of the options outlined above.
For example,

Joan Lindsay's Picnic at Hanging Rock (1967)	A823.3
Alan Duff's Once were warriors (1990)	NZ823.2
William Kirby's The golden dog (1877)	C813.4, or C823.4, or 819.134

1. The handmaid's tale, by Margaret Atwood (1939–) _____

2. The collected poems of Henry Lawson (1867–1922) _____

3. Letters of Dame Kiri Te Kanawa (1944–) _____

4. The Penguin book of great Canadian speeches _____

5. The Oxford book of New Zealand melodrama _____

6. Patrick White: a life, by David Marr (1947–) _____

EXERCISE 9.6

Break down each of the following numbers, step by step. You do not need to construct the numbers yourself.

1. Toronto writers' group anthology   C820.809 713 541

2. Australian women's writing   A820.809 287

3. Seven Canadian holiday tales   C823.010 833 4

4. New Zealand plays about monsters   NZ822.008 037

CHAPTER TEN
Number-Building—Table 4: Subdivisions of Individual Languages and Language Families
and
Table 6: Languages

Introduction
Table 4 is used with numbers from the 400 class – Language. Comprehensive resources about both language and literature are classed in the 400s.

Table 6 is used with numbers from the schedules and other tables, whenever there is an instruction to add from Table 6.

Numbers from these tables are never used alone, and they are only used at all when there is an instruction to add from the appropriate table.

The Language Class
Like the 800s, the first part of 400 is concerned with the treatment of the subject in general. 410–419 Linguistics is the science and structure of spoken and written language.

Specific languages are located in 420–490. The 400s are divided into:

400–409	Standard subdivisions and bilingualism
410–419	Linguistics
420–429	English and Old English (Anglo-Saxon)
430–439	German and related languages
440–449	French and related Romance languages
450–459	Italian, Romanian, and related languages
460–469	Spanish, Portuguese, Galician
470–479	Latin and related Italic languages
480–489	Classical Greek and related Hellenic languages
490–499	Other languages

The divisions of the 400 class follow the same pattern as the 800s. There is the same overemphasis on European languages, so that non-European languages are squeezed into one division. This results in an uneven distribution of numbers through the class, and much longer numbers for non-European language materials.

There are options to give local emphasis to a specific language. These options are not used as frequently as the options for literature. Each library has its own policy about the use of options, depending on the type of collection and the needs of its users.

Table 4

Table 4 is divided into

–01–09	Standard subdivisions
–1	Writing systems, phonology, phonetics (standard)
–2	Etymology of the standard form of the language
–3	Dictionaries of the standard form of the language
–5	Grammar of the standard form of the language
–7	Historical and geographical variations, modern nongeographical variations (dialects, slang, etc.)
–8	Standard usage of the language

 Note:

- Do not use standard subdivision –03 for dictionaries. Dictionaries are an important part of language, and have their own Table 4 number (–3).
- Phonology and phonetics deal with the sounds of a particular language.
- Etymology is concerned with the origin and history of a word.

How to Add from Table 4

1) *Determine the language.* Use the schedules (420–490) to find the base number for the language

    e.g., English   42

    Note that numbers from Table 4 can only be added to a base number, which is identified by the words 'base number' or an asterisk (*) in the schedules. If a language is not identified in the schedules as a base number, do not add from Table 4.

2) *If there is a specific aspect of the language:*
    Use Table 4 to find the number
        e.g., grammar   –5
    Add it to the base number
        e.g., English grammar   42 + 5   =   425

 For example,

    A Hungarian dictionary   494.511 3
        494.511   Hungarian language (schedules – base number)
              3   dictionary (Table 4)

    History of the Korean language   495.709
        495.7   Korean language (schedules – base number)
            09   history (Table 4 to Table 1 – standard subdivision)

EXERCISE 10.1

Check the following numbers. Find the correct number if necessary:

1.	Mind your spelling (how to spell English words)	428.1
2.	Let's learn our ABC	421.1
3.	A Chinese reader	495.1
4.	Street French: slang, idioms, and popular expletives (a historical approach)	447
5.	A crossword dictionary	423

EXERCISE 10.2

Assign DDC numbers for the following, using the schedules and Table 4:

1. The Russian alphabet   _____

2. The history of Hebrew   _____

3. A new Lao reader   _____

4. Spanish pronunciation   _____

5. Modern German slang   _____

6. Speak standard Indonesian (for native speakers)   _____

7. Teach yourself Swahili (for non-native speakers)   _____

8. English Creole dialects of the Caribbean   _____

9. Conversational New Guinea Pidgin   _____

10. Portuguese as spoken in Brazil   _____

How to Add from Table 6

Table 6 provides numbers to add whenever instructed in the schedules or other tables. This enables language to be added as an aspect of many subjects, and a second language to be added to many numbers in the 400s (e.g., a bilingual dictionary).

The numbers do not necessarily correspond to the numbers in 420–490, although the pattern is very similar. Table 6 contains:

- –1   Indo-European languages
- –2   English and Old English (Anglo-Saxon)
- –3   Germanic languages
- –4   Romance languages
- –5   Italian, Dalmatian, Romanian, Sardinian, Corsican
- –6   Spanish, Portuguese, Galician
- –7   Italic languages
- –8   Hellenic languages
- –9   Other languages

Follow the instructions to add from Table 6 whenever they occur, provided this level of specificity is appropriate for your library collection and users.

 For example,

    A Hungarian-English dictionary   494.511 321

494.511	Hungarian language (schedules – base number)
3	dictionary (table 4 –32–39)
21	English (table 6)

    The Bible in the Korean language   220.595 7

220.5	The modern Bible (schedules – base number)
957	Korean language (table 6)

 EXERCISE 10.3

Check the following numbers. Find the correct number if necessary:

1.	A quick beginners' course in Hindi for English speakers	491.438 342 1
2.	Speak Greek in a week (for English speaking people)	489.834 21
3.	Arabic phrase book (for English speaking people)	492.783
4.	Fluent English for Danish speakers	428.340 398 1
5.	A Dutch-English dictionary (one way—with entries in Dutch only)	423.393 1
6.	A Japanese-German / German-Japanese dictionary	495.631

Bilingual Dictionaries

Read carefully the instruction in Table 4 at −32–39. A distinction is made between one-way dictionaries (i.e., with entry words in only one language) and two-way dictionaries (i.e., with entry words in both languages).

EXERCISE 10.4

Assign DDC numbers for the following, using the schedules and Tables 4 and 6:

1. A French-Vietnamese dictionary   _____

2. A Khmer-English / English-Khmer dictionary   _____

3. Spanish words in the English language   _____

4. Serial publications in Tagalog   _____

5. Folk tales in Yiddish   _____

CHAPTER ELEVEN
Number-Building—Table 5: Ethnic and National Groups

Introduction
Table 5 is used to represent groups of people, and lists notation for ethnic and national groups.

Table 5 is used according to instructions that occur throughout the schedules and the other tables.

Table 5
Table 5 lists persons according to their ethnic and national origins. Numbers can be added either directly via an instruction, or indirectly by first adding –089 from Table 1 (which does not need a specific instruction). This enables the classifier to build a number for any subject studied by or in relation to any ethnic or national group.

Table 5 includes:
–1	North Americans
–2	British, English, Anglo-Saxons
–3	Germanic peoples
–4	Modern Latin peoples
–5	Italians, Romanians, related groups
–6	People who speak, or whose ancestors spoke, Spanish, Portuguese, Galician
–7	Other Italic peoples
–8	Greeks and related groups
–9	Other ethnic and national groups

Although the same European emphasis occurs in this table, it does assist the classifier to remember and locate particular numbers that appear in the schedules and several of the tables (e.g., Spanish contains –6 in the 400s, 800s, tables 2, 5 and 6).

Preference Order
Read the introduction to Table 5, that gives clear instructions as to which aspect to choose, if there is more than one in the resource. In general, ethnic group is preferred to nationality.

There are further instructions about choosing between two ethnic groups, and between two national groups.

How to Add from Table 5
With Specific Instructions

 For example,

The sociology of Australian Aboriginal people   305.899 15

1.   *Identify the base number*
        ethnic and national groups   305.8

2.   *Add from Table 5*
        Australian Aboriginals and Tasmanians   −9915

        305.8   +   −9915   =   305.899 15

Without Specific Instructions

 For example,

Australian Aboriginal sportspeople   796.089 991 5

1.   *Identify the classification number*
        athletic and outdoor sports and games   796

2.   *Check the number in the schedules for any specific instructions about standard subdivisions*
        796.01−.09 Standard subdivisions

3.   *Add −089 from Table 1*
        ethnic and national groups   −089

        796   +   −089   =   796.089

4.   *Add as instructed from Table 5*
        Australian Aboriginals and Tasmanians   −9915

        796.089   +   −9915   =   796.089 991 5

EXERCISE 11.1

Assign DDC numbers to the following subjects, using the schedules and Tables 1 and 5:

1. Social anthropology of the Kurdish people   _____

2. Social anthropology of French Canadians   _____

3. Bedouin art   _____

4. Afrikaner folk music   _____

5. Social services to Catalans   _____

6. Metal engraving of Portuguese-speaking people   _____

7. Child rearing practices of the ancient Romans   _____

8. Polynesian football players   _____

9. Rum distilled by South American native people   _____

10. Palestinian Christians   _____

EXERCISE 11.2

Assign DDC numbers to the following subjects, using the schedules and tables as required.

1. Chemistry for potters   _____

2. The ethics of teachers   _____

3. Preschool children as artists   _____

4. The art of North American native peoples   _____

5. Aerodynamics for ornithologists   _____

6. Choreography for opera singers   _____

7. An anthology of poetry by well-known detectives   _____

8. Lesbian TV stars   _____

9. Eritrean cooking in Los Angeles   _____

10. Civil and political rights in Muslim countries   _____

REVISION QUIZ 11.3

Use the following questions to revise your understanding of Tables 2 to 6. You do not need to write down the answers.

1. Can you add notation from Tables 2 to 6 to any classification number, at will?

2. Which of the auxiliary tables provide language notation?

3. Name two ways to include geographical treatment of a topic in a DDC number.

4. How does DDC's treatment of literature (the 800s and Table 3) differ from the majority of the DDC scheme?

5. What does Table 5 cover?

CHAPTER TWELVE
Number-Building—Adding from the Schedules

Introduction

Very specific numbers can be built using the auxiliary tables. DDC numbers can also be built by adding to a schedule number from elsewhere in the schedules.

Within the schedules there are many internal tables that are enumerated for one subject but apply equally to other subjects of the same type. For example, the specific topics of animals, such as behavior, genetics and so on, apply to each individual species of animal. Extra numbers are therefore listed once in the schedules, with instructions to copy this pattern for all the specific animal numbers.

There are also many numbers in the schedules, parts of which can be used with other numbers.

As with other number-building you must follow the instructions, and check the schedules when you have constructed the number to ensure that it does not conflict with another number.

Adding From the Schedules

 Here are some examples from the 900s:

987.0300223 an historical map of colonial Venezuela
987   History of Venezuela
 .03   Colonial period, 1528–1810
  00223 maps, plans, diagrams (standard subdivision, added by following the instruction "*Add as instructed under 930–990". Here we have a table of numbers to add to any of the numbers in the range 930–999 – hence 00223)

994.04005 a journal of 20th century Australian history
994   Australian history
 .04   20th century
  005 serial publication (standard subdivision, added by following the instruction "*Add as instructed under 930–990". Here we have a table of numbers to add to any of the numbers in the range 930–999 – hence 005)

919.9104   exploration of the moon
919.91   geography of the moon
      04   exploration, travel (added by following the instruction "*Add as instructed under 913–919". Here we have a table of numbers to add to any of the numbers in the range 913–919 – hence 04)

There are a number of ways to add from another part of the schedules.

Adding a Direct Number from Another Part of the Schedules

eg   For example,
        Agricultural libraries   026.63

1.   *Identify the base number*
            Libraries ... devoted to specific subjects   026

2.   *Follow the 'Add' instruction at .001–.999 Specific subjects*
            "Add to base number 026 notation 001–999"

3.   *Add any number in the schedules between 001 and 999*
            e.g., agriculture   630
                    026   +   630   =   026.63

Adding Part of a Number

eg   For example,
        Secondary education for social responsibility   373.011 5

1.   *Identify the base number*
            373.011 secondary education for specific objectives

2.   *Add the numbers following 370.11 in 370.111–370.119 ...*
        Look at the range 370.111–370.119
        Find the number with the same aspect we are looking for
            e.g., 370.115   education for social responsibility
        Write down the number 370.115
        The instruction states 'numbers following 370.11'
        Draw a line after 370.11

            e.g., 370.11 | 5 – this is the only number we want

            So, secondary education for social responsibility
                    373.011   +   5   =   373.011 5

Adding from a Table in the Schedules

These tables can only be used when directed. The numbers to which they can be added are usually indicated by an asterisk (*) or a dagger (†).

    For example,
Breeding racehorses   636.122

1.   *Identify the classification number*
        e.g., racehorses   636.12*

2.   *Follow instructions at the asterisk (*)*
        e.g., *Add as instructed under 636.1–636.8

3.   *Add from the table at 636.1–636.8*
        e.g., breeding   2
                636.12   +   2   =   636.122

 EXERCISE 12.1

What do the following DDC numbers represent?

1.   940.316 2   _____

2.   025.171 6   _____

3.   255.530 09   _____

4.   725.210 87   _____

5.   782.107 941   _____

EXERCISE 12.2

Assign DDC numbers to the following subjects, using the schedules and tables as required:

1. Financial journalists and journalism   _____

2. Snakes in the Bible   _____

3. Commerce in the Koran   _____

4. Conversion of non-Jews to Judaism in India   _____

5. Diseases in corn crops   _____

6. Restoration of commercial buildings   _____

7. Care of games in libraries   _____

8. Learning about crocodiles from museums   _____

9. Scientific works as literature   _____

10. Raising goats as stunt animals   _____

CHAPTER THIRTEEN
WebDewey

Introduction

WebDewey is a Web-based version of the Dewey Decimal Classification, developed to maximize the usefulness of the scheme through the capacity to search electronically. As well as the classification scheme contained in the four printed volumes, it provides additional features including mappings to various subject heading schemes, authority records for DDC numbers with corresponding Library of Congress subject headings, and the ability to record comments and customize screen displays.

Learning to Use WebDewey

It is easier to use WebDewey if you already have an overall grasp of the scheme, especially the hierarchy and the procedure for building numbers. If you are new to DDC, refer to earlier chapters of this book to gain an understanding of the structure before you begin to use WebDewey.

OCLC provides a free tutorial, *WebDewey 2.0: an overview* on its website. The tutorial can be accessed at www.oclc.org/dewey/resources/tutorial.html. It introduces you to searching and browsing, teaches you how to create user notes, and shows you how to build DDC numbers using WebDewey.

Features and Options

Users can create and store their own notes, whether they refer to the general practice of their library or relate to a specific topic and/or Dewey number.

By entering a library catalog's URL, a user can send a search from any Dewey number to the catalog's call number index.

There are two basic options for searching WebDewey: Search and Browse. Several indexes are available for each option. Over time you will establish your preferred approach. Sharing techniques with colleagues who use WebDewey will be invaluable to you.

Access to WebDewey is part of OCLC's fee-based cataloging service. If you can log in to WebDewey via your library, the following exercises will introduce you to the most common search options.

WebDewey Search

 Example: Manufacturing outdoor furniture

1. In the **Search** box – enter 'outdoor furniture'. Leave the **All Fields** index selected. Click **Search** (or press Enter).

2. The terms displayed are:

    1. 392.36   Dwelling places
    2. 645.4   Furniture and accessories
    3. 645.8   Outdoor furnishings
    4. 648.5   Housecleaning
    5. 684.12–684.16   Specific kinds of furniture
    6. 684.18   Outdoor furniture
    7. 749.3   Specific kinds of furniture
    8. 749.8   Outdoor furniture

3. Identify the likely numbers.

4. Click on '684.18 Outdoor furniture' for closer examination.

5. You can see the hierarchy, notes, and Relative Index term. (Terms from various subject heading schemes are also given if they have been mapped to the DDC number.)

6. This looks like the right number. Choose 684.18.

EXERCISE 13.1

*Assign DDC numbers to the following topics using the **Search** option:*

1. A guide to coffee table design   _____

2. Growing begonias   _____

3. The law of income tax   _____

4. Aerial photography   _____

5. Upholstering your sofa   _____

6. Causes of unemployment   _____

7. Journalism in Moscow   _____

8. Modern British sheep breeds   _____

9. Modern art   _____

10. Church architecture   _____

WebDewey Browse

 Example: Social class

1. Click on the **Browse** button at the top of the screen

2. In the **Browse for** box – enter 'social class'. Choose the **Relative Index**. Click **Search** (or press Enter).

3. The terms displayed are:

Social choice	302.13
Social classes	T1--0862
Social classes	305.5
Social classes *see Manual at* 305.9 vs. 305.5	
Social classes--civil rights	323.322
Social classes--customs	390.2
Social classes--dress	391.02
Social classes--dwellings	392.36086
Social classes--Koran	279.12283055
Social classes--relations with government	323.322
Social classes--religion	200.862
Social classes--religion--Christianity	270.0862
Social classes--social welfare	362.892

4. Click on any of the numbers to see an expansion of the hierarchy, notes, Relative Index terms and subject headings.

5. Click on the link to the Manual to see a discussion of the use of the two numbers shown.

6. Choose the number that best suits the emphasis in the resource you are classifying.

EXERCISE 13.2

*Assign DDC numbers to the following topics using the **Browse** option:*

1. Etruscan sculpture   _____

2. Dinosaurs   _____

3. Halley's comet   _____

4. A history of drug addiction   _____

5. Having twins : a parent's guide to pregnancy, birth
    and early childhood   _____

6. Chemical contraception   _____

7. Educating children with communicative disorders   _____

8. Sports injuries   _____

9. Fashion modelling   _____

10. Bringing up children   _____

EXERCISE 13.3

*Check the following DDC numbers, and correct them if necessary, using the **Browse** option. For example, is the following number correct?*

Radio advertising   659.1402

1. In the **Browse for** box – enter '659.1402'. Choose **Dewey Numbers (with Captions)**. Click **Search** (or press Enter).

2. The terms displayed include:

659.14	Advertising in electronic media
659.1402	No partial match, see nearby terms
659.142	Radio
659.143	Television
659.144	Advertising in digital media
659.15	Display advertising
659.152	Exhibitions and shows
659.157	Point-of-sale advertising

3. There is no matching caption, and 659.1402 says 'No partial match, see nearby terms'

4. 659.142 is the number for radio advertising. Click on 'Radio' to see an expansion of the hierarchy, and the Relative Index term.

5. It is clear that 659.1402 is incorrect. Choose 659.142 as the correct term.

1.	The Crusades	909.07
2.	The Apostles' Creed	238.11
3.	Rhymes and rhyming games	398.84
4.	Xhosa language	496.39805
5.	Forecasting storms	551.6425

CHAPTER FOURTEEN
More Practice

EXERCISE 14.1
What do the following DDC numbers represent?

1. 005.382 _____

2. 070.593 _____

3. 133.54 _____

4. 155.937 _____

5. 268.67 _____

6. 303.484 _____

7. 920.72 _____

8. 590.734 6 _____

9. 428.42 _____

10. 423.15 _____

11. 509.2 _____

12. 428.405 _____

13. 658.45 _____

14. 786.509 2 _____

15. 796.358 082 _____

EXERCISE 14.2

Assign DDC numbers to the following subjects:

1. Thailand: description and travel _____

2. Central Australia: discovery and exploration (1795–1869) _____

3. City of Adelaide (S.A.): description and travel in the 1930s _____

4. Asia: description and travel in the 1980s _____

5. Bahrain: travel in the twentieth century _____

6. Natural monuments in Australia: a pictorial view _____

7. The Readers' Digest guide to the coasts of Victoria, Tasmania and South Australia (designed to show points of interest in the 1980s) _____

8. A guidebook for travel in Sydney _____

9. A guidebook for travel in Colorado _____

10. Geographic features of ancient Rhodes _____

11. Travel in India during 318–500 AD _____

12. Prehistoric geography of Carthage _____

13. Maps of Yellowstone National Park _____

14. Maps of the Hunter Valley of N.S.W. _____

15. Atlas of the ancient world _____

EXERCISE 14.3

Assign DDC numbers to the following subjects:

1. Atlas of the oceans of the world   _____

2. Physical geography of mountains   _____

3. An illustrated atlas of islands   _____

4. Maps of the Pacific Ocean in the 18th century   _____

5. Maps of the ancient Roman Empire   _____

6. Spiritualism in Catholic countries   _____

7. Trade unions in Malaysia   _____

8. Social welfare services to the mentally ill in British Columbia   _____

9. A guide to the snakes of Ireland   _____

10. Rail passenger transport in Belgium   _____

11. Printmaking in France   _____

12. Water birds of the world   _____

13. Local government in the Southern Hemisphere   _____

14. Birds of the Indian Ocean   _____

15. A guide to wine making in New Zealand   _____

EXERCISE 14.4

Assign DDC numbers to the following subjects:

1.   Transplants in Transylvania   _____

2.   The paintings of Tom Roberts (Australian)   _____

3.   Postage stamps of Angola   _____

4.   Country music from Texas   _____

5.   Horse racing tracks in Hong Kong   _____

6.   Horse riding in the Australian Capital Territory   _____

7.   Hunting in South Africa in the nineteenth century   _____

8.   German Christian church architecture of the sixteenth century _____

9.   The *Sydney Morning Herald* & other Sydney newspapers   _____

10. Folk songs of Chile   _____

11. Dutch narrative poetry   _____

12. Spanish farce   _____

13. Twentieth-century Spanish drama   _____

14. The modern Indonesian novel – the works of Pramoedya
     Ananta Toer (20th century)   _____

15. An Indonesian dictionary   _____

EXERCISE 14.5

Assign DDC numbers to the following subjects:

1.   English-Indonesian dictionary _____

2.   English-Indonesian-English dictionary _____

3.   Dictionary of Indonesian acronyms _____

4.   Use of French words in English _____

5.   English for Spanish people _____

6.   English for Malayalam-speaking people _____

7.   Choral singing for the hearing impaired _____

8.   Case histories in psychiatry _____

9.   Pasteur the chemist: a biography _____

10. General biology: a quarterly magazine _____

11. A guide to fascist political theory _____

12. Harraps Russian dictionary _____

13. The Roman Catholic Church in Spain _____

14. The journal of sports medicine _____

15. Kenya before the British _____

EXERCISE 14.6

Assign DDC numbers to the following subjects:

1. How to read maps   _____

2. Makeup for pantomime   _____

3. The ethics of euthanasia   _____

4. Biographies of ancient Egyptians   _____

5. Biographies of notable Canadians   _____

6. The movement for women's suffrage   _____

7. The Pankhursts: a biography of suffragettes   _____

8. Modern archaeology: techniques and equipment   _____

9. Genealogical sources of Scotland   _____

10. An introduction to historiography   _____

11. Aboriginal Dreamtime stories   _____

12. Erotica in art   _____

13. Design of caravan parks for long-term residents   _____

14. An introduction to pumps   _____

15. Dictionary of biology   _____

EXERCISE 14.7

Assign DDC numbers to the following subjects:

1. Dutch poetry of the 17th century   _____

2. The design of motels for the aged   _____

3. First aid for gunshot wounds   _____

4. Scotland under James II   _____

5. Modern joinery: a guide to Scandinavian practices   _____

6. The spiritual discipline of yoga   _____

7. Scale models of solar-powered automotive engines   _____

8. Manufacture of toilet tissue: patents   _____

9. Research in the engineering design of hand tools   _____

10. Underwriting health and accident insurance   _____

11. English fiction: a secondary school study guide   _____

12. The Bathurst prison riot   _____

13. Auckland Art Gallery   _____

14. The design of tug boats   _____

15. A zoological study of clams, mussels & cuttlefish   _____

EXERCISE 14.8

What do the following DDC numbers represent?

1.   549.911 _____

2.   513.071 2 _____

3.   634.709 94 _____

4.   853.914 _____

5.   912.944 1 _____

6.   978.112 5 _____

7.   025.065 786 809 946 _____

8.   004.015 1 _____

9.   285.295 95 _____

10. 296.830 994 51 _____

11. 305.488 992 109 4 _____

12. 324.630 899 915 _____

13. 338.274 309 959 2 _____

14. 362.102 308 2 _____

15. 378.33 _____

EXERCISE 14.9

Assign DDC numbers to the following subjects:

1. Traditional Jewish rites: Bar mitzvah _____

2. Research into the manufacture of synthetic perfumes _____

3. Collecting pistols _____

4. The waterfalls of Hawaii: a description _____

5. Translating biochemical material _____

6. Corals of the Australian Barrier Reef _____

7. Canada under Trudeau _____

8. The building of rock fill dams in the 19th century _____

9. Nursing psychiatric patients _____

10. Nebraska between the World Wars _____

11. Residential care for heroin addicts _____

12. Prostitution in the 20th century: a sociological study _____

13. Photographs of animals _____

14. Rotary clubs in Arizona _____

15. The mining of tin _____

EXERCISE 14.10

What do the following DDC numbers represent?

1.   181.07 _____

2.   153.947 96 _____

3.   155.911 67 _____

4.   428.340 709 4 _____

5.   331.124 15 _____

6.   331.137 810 027 4 _____

7.   331.119 166 _____

8.   331.252 959 _____

9.   331.413 7 _____

10. 338.372 751 _____

11. 336.266 73 _____

12. 230.98 _____

13. 220.520 33 _____

14. 230.071 185 _____

15. 220.872 582 704 72 _____

EXERCISE ANSWERS

EXERCISE 1.1
Our world is classified by an infinite number of schemes, from the organization of supermarket shelves to scientific classification of species and subspecies to the grouping and ranking of employees in the workplace, whether by qualifications, duties performed, salary and/or status and so on.

EXERCISE 1.2
Possible criteria for organizing your 'zoo' include:
geographic origin—e.g., all the African animals in one place
habitat—e.g., all the tropical animals together
species—e.g., all the birds together
diet—e.g., all the carnivores together.

The point of the exercise is for you to see that there is more than one way of grouping objects (topics) together. Questions to consider include whether your scheme is able to accommodate all the animals and whether it provides a reasonably even distribution of animals. Once you have decided on your criteria, it is important to be consistent.

REVISION QUIZ 1.3
1. The primary reason is to arrange items on the library shelves according to their subject content.
    Other reasons include:
    *   bringing related items together in a helpful sequence;
    *   providing formal orderly access to the shelves either through a direct search of the shelves (browsing) or via the catalog;
    *   enabling easy reshelving of library materials; and
    *   providing an order for the classified catalog.

2. Enumerative classification attempts to spell out (enumerate) all the single and composite subject concepts required—e.g., Library of Congress Classification, Dewey Decimal Classification (to a lesser extent).
    Synthetic classification lists numbers for single concepts, and allows the classifier to construct (synthesise) numbers for composite subjects—e.g., Colon Classification, Universal Decimal Classification, some features of DDC.

3. Classification schedules are arranged in number order. This enables the classifier to see the relationships between topics, and to find closely related numbers.

4. Number building is the construction of classification numbers not listed in the schedules, following rules given in the scheme. It allows for more specific numbers to be created, and saves a great deal of space in the schedules.

5. Hierarchical classification is classification in which the division of subjects is from the most general to the most specific. Each number is included in the number above it in the hierarchy, so that each subordinate subject is classified at a more specific number within the same hierarchy.

6. Since the primary purpose of classification is to group resources according to their subject content in order to facilitate their access and use, it is important to consider who are the users, and what organization of material is most useful to them.

EXERCISE 2.1

615.954	361
616	361.003
616.09	361.02
616.11	361.04
616.122	361.1
616.123	361.103
616.1237	361.2
616.125	361.23
616.200435	361.3
616.2009	361.301
616.201	361.32
616.24	361.3205
616.240083	361.320994
616.241	361.322
616.244	361.32205
617.0083	361.37
617.08	361.37025
617.44	361.3703
617.80083	

REVISION QUIZ 2.2

1. Dewey Decimal Classification is divided into ten main classes. These are each divided into ten divisions, each of which is divided into ten sections.

2. The Relative Index relates topics to all of their aspects, by showing all the numbers for a topic in the different disciplines to which they belong—e.g.,

    Mothers
family relationships	306.874 3
guides to Christian life	248.843 1
psychology	155.646 3

3. The advantages of DDC include:
    *   DDC was the first to use the concept of relative location to organize materials on the shelf.
    *   The pure notation (i.e., all Arabic numbers) is recognized internationally.
    *   The straightforward numerical sequence facilitates filing and shelving.
    *   The Relative Index brings together different aspects of the same subject that are scattered in different disciplines.

- The hierarchical notation expresses the relationship between and among class numbers.
- The decimal system in theory enables infinite expansion and subdivision.
- The mnemonic notation helps users to memorize and recognize class numbers.
- Periodic revision keeps it up-to-date.

4.   The disadvantages of DDC include:
- Its Anglo-American bias is evident in its emphasis on American, English and European language, literature and history in the 400s, 800s and 900s, Protestantism/Christianity in the 200s.
- Some related disciplines are separated: 400 / 800, 300 / 900.
- Some subjects are not very comfortably placed—e.g., Library science in 000; Psychology as part of Philosophy in 100; Sports and amusements in 700.
- In the 800s, literary works by the same author are scattered according to form.
- Decimal numbering limits its capacity for accommodating subjects on the same level—e.g., there can only be 9 divisions (+ 1 general division).
- Different rates of growth of some disciplines have resulted in an uneven structure—e.g., 300 and 600 are particularly overcrowded.
- Although theoretically expansion is infinite, it doesn't allow infinite insertion between related numbers—e.g., between 610 and 619.
- Specificity results in long numbers that can be awkward for shelving and on spine labels.
- Re-locations create practical problems in libraries—e.g., the need for re-classification, re-labelling, and re-shelving.

EXERCISE 3.1

1.   Epilepsy — 1, 2, 5
2.   Art — 1, 2, 5, 9
3.   Astrology — 1, 2, 5
4.   Whichever of fishing and boating comes first in DDC — 1, 2, 7
5.   Social sciences — 1, 2, 3
6.   Japanese fiction — 1, 4
7.   This could be any one of a wide range of subjects, including psychology, philosophy, religion, anatomy — 1, 2, 5, 10
8.   Geography of Seattle — 1, 2, 5, 6
9.   World literature — 1, 2, 4
10.   Geography of Italy, or, urban planning in Italy — 1, 2, 9
11.   Bible — 1, 2, 5
12.   Inflation, then Bolivia — 1, 2, 5, 12
13.   Whichever of apples and pears comes first in DDC — 1, 2, 7
14.   Apples — 1, 2, 5
15.   Fruit — 1, 2, 5, 9
16.   Stone fruit — 1, 2, 5, 9
17.   Berry fruit — 1, 2, 14
18.   Painting, then landscape painting, then Scotland — 1, 2, 5, 13
19.   Composting, then Australia and New Zealand — 1, 2, 5, 16
20.   Religion — 1, 2, 5

EXERCISE 3.2

Subject	Classification Heading	Broad / Close
Physical therapies	Physical therapies	close
Marital relationship	Marriage & family	broad
Rome's history	History of Italy	broad
Marriage counselling	Family problems & services	broad
Business law	Law	broad
Modern French Bible	Modern language Bibles	broad
The Shakers (religious group)	Adherents of religious groups	broad
Blood	Blood	close
Banking in Thailand	Thai banks & banking	close
Christian Church's views on sex, marriage & family	Christian attitudes on sex, marriage & family	broad or close, depending on whether you think the Church's attitudes = Christian attitudes

REVISION QUIZ 3.3

1.   As much as is needed to be confident of what it is about.

2.   Since DDC is based on disciplines, you need to decide in which discipline the subject belongs.

3.   Broad classification uses the main divisions and subdivisions of a scheme without breaking down into narrower concepts.
Close classification means classifying each item as specifically as possible, using all available subdivisions in the classification scheme.
e.g.,   for a resource on growing apples in Tasmania,
the number for fruit-growing is broad classification;
apple-growing in Tasmania is close classification.

4.   Citation order is the order in which you are instructed to add different aspects of a subject.
Preference order is the order in which to choose one aspect when a subject has more than one aspect, but the rules allow only one to be added.
They are different, since citation order allows more than one aspect to be reflected, whereas preference requires a choice to be made.

5.   A call number usually consists of a classification number, a book number and often a location symbol. It is the number on a library item that shows where it is located.

6.   Stocktaking can be done by reading the barcodes on the items with a wand, and using the online catalog to compare this information with its database.
Classification numbers can be checked direct from the catalog.
Subject bibliographies can be produced from the catalog.
The catalog can be used for insurance purposes, as a record of the library's holdings.

EXERCISE 4.1

1.	My book of opera	700
2.	A child's Bible	200
3.	Three Irish plays	800
4.	World book encyclopedia	000
5.	Teach yourself Vietnamese	400
6.	The psychology of violence	100
7.	Russian rockets	600
8.	Physics for beginners	500
9.	Road atlas of New Zealand	900
10.	Employment of aged persons	300
11.	Multicultural education	300
12.	Encyclopaedia of Papua New Guinea	900
13.	How to draw cartoons	700
14.	Introductory philosophy	100
15.	Agricultural pest control	600

EXERCISE 4.2

1.	Audiovisual materials in libraries	020
2.	Japanese printmaking	760
3.	Growing wheat for export	630
4.	Twentieth century architecture	720
5.	A concise history of Chile	980
6.	The nursing handbook	610
7.	Palaeontological studies	560
8.	Encouraging women into politics	320
9.	A historical atlas of ancient Egypt	910 or 930
10.	Carnivorous plants	580
11.	The Methodist Church in the Pacific	270 or 280
12.	Abortion	(ethics) 170 or (medicine) 610 or (services) 360
13.	The planet Mars	520
14.	How to play hockey	790
15.	Learn Polish : an audiovisual approach	490
16.	The Oxford dictionary	420
17.	Caring for rare books	090
18.	Child psychology	150
19.	The legal handbook	340
20.	Jewish folk tales	390

EXERCISE 4.3

1.	Developing educational curricula	375
2.	Harrap's new German grammar	435
3.	The plays of William Shakespeare	822
4.	Electricity	537
5.	Let's visit Kenya	916
6.	The philosophy of Socrates	183
7.	South-East Asian cooking	641

8.	What bird is that?	598
9.	Journalism in the new Russia	077
10.	Steam trains for enthusiasts	625 or 385
11.	Islam	297
12.	Introduction to trout fishing	799

EXERCISE 4.4

1. 900 is superordinate to <u>all the other numbers (930, 938, 938.03)</u>.
2. 930 is <u>subordinate</u> to 900.
3. <u>938.03</u> is subordinate to 938.

REVISION QUIZ 4.5

1. The First, Second and Third Summaries list the main classes, divisions and sections with their headings. They are used to become familiar with the overall structure of DDC, and to locate numbers that relate to each other.

2. Disciplines form the basic structure of DDC. In the DDC, subjects are arranged by disciplines.

3. Hierarchy is the arrangement of subjects, and the numbers that represent them, in a structure where more specific subjects are part of, and subordinate to, broader subjects. It is fundamental to DDC, since it allows the classifier to find specific numbers in their relationship with more general ones.

4. 155 is superordinate to 155.4. This means that '155 Differential and developmental psychology' includes '155.4 Child psychology', or that '155.4 Child psychology' is part of '155 Differential and developmental psychology'.

5. It is likely to be a very specific number. Each number that is subordinate to another number is one digit longer. Therefore the more specific the subject, the longer the number.

6. The auxiliary tables enable more specific numbers to be made, by adding a particular aspect of a subject to a number from the schedules. For example, the number for an encyclopedia of folklore is constructed by adding –03 (dictionaries, encyclopedias, concordances) from Table 1 to 398 (Folklore) to give 398.03.

7. No. Although the index is very comprehensive, it does not include all the aspects of all possible subjects—e.g., American short stories, educational statistics.

8. The interdisciplinary number for helicopters is 387.733 52.

9. The Manual (in Volume 1) gives an explanation at '550 *vs.* 910'

10. The Glossary (in Volume 1) gives the definition: 'The rule instructing that works that give equal treatment to three or more subjects that are all subdivisions of a broader subject are classified in the first higher number that includes all of them'. For example, a resource on growing coconuts, avocados and papayas is classified at the number for growing tropical and subtropical fruits.

EXERCISE 5.1

1.   An illustrated history of 15th century Japan
        Main subject: History of Japan
        Secondary aspect: 15th century
        Secondary aspect: illustrated

2.   A dictionary of terms for motorists
        Main subject: Motoring
        Secondary aspect: dictionary

3.   The history of glass-blowing in Venice in the Middle Ages
        Main subject: Glass-blowing
        Secondary aspect: history
        Secondary aspect: in Venice
        Secondary aspect: in the Middle Ages

EXERCISE 5.2

1.   Class: 000   Specific term(s): Keyword indexing / KWIC indexing / KWOC indexing
                DDC number: 025.486

2.   Class: 300   Specific term(s): Disposal of dead *see also* Undertaking (Mortuary) – law
                DDC number: 344.045 (because this covers law aspects. not 363.75, which focuses
                on disposal as a public /social service)

3.   Class: 300   Specific term(s): Home care services   DDC number: 362.14
      or
      Class: 600   Specific term(s): Home care services 362.14 *see also 649.8 for home care by family
                members*   DDC number: 649.8

      or
      Class: 600   Specific term(s): Nursing   DDC number: 610.7343

4.   Class: 100   Specific term(s): Homosexuality – ethics   DDC number: 176
      or
      Class: 200   Specific term(s): Homosexuality – ethics – religion   DDC number: 205.664
                (comparative religion), 294.356 64 (Buddhism), 241.664 (Christianity), 294.548
                664 (Hinduism), 296.3664 (Judaism)

5.   Class: 900   Specific term(s): Twelve Tribes   DDC number: 933.02

6.   Class: 600   Specific term(s): Adobe – building construction   DDC number: 693.22
      or
      Class: 700   Specific term(s): Adobe – architectural construction   DDC number: 721.044 22

7.   Class: 300   Specific term(s): Blood banks   DDC number: 362.178 4

8.   Class: 200   Specific term(s): God – Islam   DDC number: 297.211

9.   Class: 500   Specific term(s): Volcanoes   DDC number: 551.21

10.   Class: 300   Specific term(s): Family counseling   DDC number: 362.828 6

11.   Class: 100   Specific term(s): Perception – psychology   DDC number: 153.7
       or
       Class: 100   Specific term(s): Perception – psychology – sensory   DDC number: 152.1
       (*see Manual at 153.7 vs. 152.1*)

12.   Class: 100   Specific term/s: Philosophers – eastern, or, Ancient philosophy
       DDC number: 181.11

13.   Class: 300   Specific term/s: Toys – product safety   DDC number: 363.19
       or
       Class: 300   Specific term/s: Hazardous materials – public safety   DDC number: 363.19 (index
       indicates 363.17, but note says: '363.17 *For hazardous materials as components
       of articles that become hazardous products, see 363.19*')

14.   Class: 700   Specific term/s: School buildings *see also Educational buildings.*   Educational
       buildings – architecture   DDC number: 727

15.   Class: 900   Specific term/s: World War II   DDC number: 940.531 1

EXERCISE 6.1

1.   **345.072**   **Pretrial procedures in criminal law**
      300   Social sciences
      340   Law
      345   Criminal law
      345.07   Trials
      345.072   Pretrial procedure

2.   **659.143**   **Television advertising**
      600   Technology (Applied sciences)
      650   Management and auxiliary services
      659   Advertising and public relations
      659.1   Advertising
      659.14   Advertising in electronic media
      659.143   Television

3.   **375.001**   **Curriculum development**
      300   Social sciences
      370   Education
      375   Curricula
      375.001   Curriculum development

4. **599.972   Origins and causes of physical differences among ethnic groups**
    500   Natural sciences and mathematics
    590   Animals
    599   Mammalia (Mammals)
    599.9   Homo sapiens (Humans)
    599.97   Human ethnic groups
    599.972   Origins and causes of physical differences among ethnic groups

5. **910.452   Accounts of shipwrecks**
    900   History, geography and auxiliary disciplines
    910   Geography and travel
    910.4   Accounts of travel and facilities for travelers
    910.45   Ocean travel and seafaring adventures
    910.452   Shipwrecks

EXERCISE 6.2

There are hundreds (thousands?) of examples of each of these. One example of each is provided here — you only need to check the answers given if you were unable to find an example, or are not sure whether you correctly understand the term.

1. *A heading*:   400 Language

2. *A summary:*   see the First, Second and Third Summaries at the beginning of Volume 2

3. *A centered heading:*   > 180–190 History, geographic treatment, biography

4. *A subordinate number:*   '394.6 Fairs' is subordinate to '394 General customs'

5. *A relocated topic:*   721[.042] Buildings by shape, buildings with atriums
                                        Relocated to 72048

6. *A class-elsewhere note:* 728.1 Low-cost housing
                                        Class specific types of low-cost housing in 728.3–728.7

7. *A see also reference:*   641.5636 Vegetarian cooking
                                        See also 641.65 for cooking vegetables

8. *A see reference:*   741 Drawing and drawings
                                        For drawing and drawings by subject, see 743

9. *A scope note:*   022 Administration of physical plant (of libraries)
                                        Including bookmobiles

10. *An option:*   810–890 Literatures of specific languages and language families
                              Literature is classed by the language in which originally written
                              (Option: Class translations into a language requiring local emphasis
                              with the literature of that language)

EXERCISE 6.3

1. 621.3276   Sodium-vapor lighting
    621.324   Gas lighting
    628.95   Public lighting
    None of the numbers covers all aspects of the subject. The correct number could be 621.3276—Sodium-vapor lighting or 628.95—Public lighting, depending on whether 'sodium-vapor' or 'public' was more important.

2. 788.94   French horns
    681.8   (Manufacture of) Musical instruments
    736.6   Carving ivory, bone, horn, shell, amber
    736.6—Carving ivory, bone, horn, shell, amber most closely classifies the subject.

3. 398.3   Real phenomena as subjects of folklore
    398.365   Minerals (as subjects of folklore)
    549.23   Metals (Mineralogy)
    739.22   Goldsmithing (Art metalwork)
    553.41   Formation and structure of gold deposits
    398.365—Minerals as subjects of folklore most closely classifies the subject.

4. 364.44   Welfare services in the prevention of crime and delinquency
    362.88   Problems of and services to victims of crimes and war
    363.23   Police functions as part of Social problems and services
        (Class here prevention of crime by police)
    365.46   (Penal and related) institutions for the criminally insane
    362.88—Problems of and services to victims of crime most closely classifies the subject (unless another aspect is particularly emphasised).

5. 665.5384   Technology of heavy fuel oil (Including absorber oil, diesel fuel, gas oil, heating oil)
    621.4025   Equipment for heat engineering
    644.1   Heating (Household utilities)
    644.1—Heating (Household utilities) most closely classifies the subject.

6. 616.12   Diseases of the heart
    617.412   Heart surgery
    641.56311 Cooking for persons with heart disease
    614.5912   Incidence of and public measures to prevent heart disease
    614.5912—Incidence of and public measures to prevent heart disease most closely classifies the subject.

EXERCISE 6.4

1.	The history of the Punic wars	937.04
2.	An introduction to photochemistry	541.35
3.	Big game hunting	799.26
4.	How valleys are formed	551.442
5.	The ouija board in spiritualism	133.932 5
6.	The identification of waterbirds	598.176
7.	How to read maps	912.014
8.	The Lutheran Church in America	284.133
9.	New ideas in tax reform	336.205

10. Unemployment resulting from technological change   331.137 042
11. Cycle racing   796.62
12. Behaviour of people in disasters   155.935
13. Electricity from the wind   621.312 136 or 333.92
14. Cleaning clothes at home   648.1
15. Sculpture in wax and wood   731.2

EXERCISE 6.5

1.   Ethiopia under Italian rule   963.057
2.   Drawing and preparing maps   526
3.   Social responsibility of executive management   658.408
4.   Talismans in witchcraft   133.44
5.   Rules of Parliament   060.42 or 328.1
6.   Detergent technology   668.14
7.   Military intelligence   355.343 2
8.   Ultrasonic vibrations   (physics)   534.55 or (engineering) 620.28
9.   Design of roadworks   (engineering)   625.725 or (area planning) 711.73
10. Sculpture in the twentieth century   735.23
11. Plant diseases   571.92 or 632.3
12. Speed drills for typing   652.307
13. The ethics of government   172.2
14. Music for the guitar   787.87
15. Discipline in the classroom   371.102 4
16. Zodiac: an astrological guide   133.52
17. Making trousers commercially   687.116
18. Looking after hawks and falcons   636.686 9

EXERCISE 6.6

1.   A general introduction to the violin, cello and other
     bowed string instruments   787
2.   Design and construction of clocks   681.113
3.   Cookery in restaurants   641.572
4.   How to code computer programs   005.13
5.   The use of radio in adult education   374.26
6.   Evolution of microbes   579.138
7.   Growing carrots in the home garden   635.13
8.   Techniques for indoor photography   778.72
9.   Eighteenth century sculpture   735.21
10. Manufacture of paper   676
11. Triplets, quads and more: an obstetric guide   618.25
12. The Panama Canal: modern aid to transportation   386.44
13. The physics of auroras   538.768
14. Flying fishes and silversides: odd marine creatures 597.66
15. A guide to cooking with pressure cookers   641.587

EXERCISE 7.1

1.	Dictionary of child psychology	155.403
2.	Journal of manufacture of electronic toys	688.728 05
3.	The language of soccer	796.334 014
4.	Pony weekly magazine	636.160 5
5.	Teaching netball	796.324 071
6.	The philosophy of idealism	141
7.	The philosophy of social work	361.301
8.	Standards for lathes	621.942 021 8
9.	Dictionary of biochemistry	572.03
10.	A history of child care	649.109
11.	Systems of long-range weather forecasting	551.636 501 1
12.	Sales catalogue of wedding dresses	392.540 29
13.	Guidebook for a toy museum	745.592 074
14.	The terrier encyclopaedia	636.755 03
15.	Genetics research	576.507 2
16.	Handicrafts for people with disabilities	745.508 7

EXERCISE 7.2

The titles given are examples. Other titles covering the same topics are equally correct.

1.	796.35205	Golf monthly
2.	370.3	The education encyclopedia
		(the title 'A dictionary of education' would be just as correct for this number)
3.	371.003	A dictionary of school and special education
		(the title 'The encyclopedia of school and special education' would be just as correct for this number)
4.	372.03	A dictionary of elementary education
5.	375.0003	A dictionary of curricula
6.	629.1323005	Aerodynamics quarterly
7.	181.005	The journal of Oriental philosophy
8.	336.00285	Data processing in public finance
9.	621.3880072	Television research and development
10.	730.74	Sculpture museums
11.	300.724	Experimental research in the social sciences
12.	512.005	The journal of algebra
13.	512.705	The journal of number theory
14.	338.4300072	Industry investment research

EXERCISE 7.3

1.	Dictionary of library and information science	020.3
2.	Philosophy of library science	020.1
3.	Library and information science: a journal	020.5
4.	Dictionary of psychology	150.3
5.	Psychology: historical research	150.722
6.	Dictionary of ethics	170.3
7.	Ethics: a quarterly journal	170.5

8.	International architecture organisations	720.601
9.	Dictionary of architecture	720.3
10.	Study and teaching of chemical technology	660.071

EXERCISE 7.4

1.	Popular engineering (quarterly journal)	620.005
2.	Agricultural pest control monthly	632.905
3.	Apparatus used in puppetry	791.530 284
4.	Correspondence courses in electronics	621.381 071 5
5.	Songs of the Middle Ages	782.420 902
6.	Encyclopedia of horses	599.665 503 or 636.100 3
7.	History of the social sciences	300.9
8.	Philosophy of Christianity	230.01
9.	Historical research into public administration	351.072 2
10.	Lives of ten great artists	700.922
11.	Theory of the solar system	523.201
12.	Research in oceanography	551.460 72
13.	Harness racing news (monthly journal)	798.460 5
14.	Theory of personnel management	658.300 1
15.	Book publishing trade catalogues *(see note at 070.5029)*	015
16.	Journal of the philosophy of socialism *(see Manual entry for choice of 335 over 320.53)*	335.001

REVISION QUIZ 7.5

1. Standard subdivisions enable the classifier to make the number more specific by representing a regularly-recurring form or treatment as well as the main subject.

2. They can almost always be added freely, when needed, to any classification number, although only one is added for any one resource.

3. The number is shown as T1—.

4. When the number is already built into the schedules.
   When they would be redundant, because the number already covers the concept of the standard subdivision.
   When there is an instruction not to use the standard subdivisions.
   When the subject of the resource is more specific than the classification number.
   When there is an 'including' note at a number.

5. −01   Philosophy and theory
   −03   Dictionaries, encyclopedias, concordances
   −05   Serial publications
   −07   Education, research, related topics
   −09   Historical, geographic treatment, biography.

6. To ensure that these 'standard' treatments of the subject can be shelved in their groups before the subject is further subdivided.

7. There are many numbers that have a non-standard procedure for the use of standard subdivisions.

8.   335.003

9.   The table at the beginning of Table 1, that indicates which standard subdivision to use if there is more than one possible standard subdivision representing different aspects of the topic.

10.   −0284, that comes before −07 in the table of preference.

EXERCISE 8.1

1.	The geography of Zimbabwe	916.891
2.	A textbook of Papua New Guinea geography	919.53
3.	The Amazon River: a geography	918.11
4.	Geography of ancient Rhodes	913.916
5.	A hotel guide to the French Riviera	914.494 06
6.	The travellers' guide to Spain	914.604
7.	Prehistoric geography of Carthage	913.973 01
8.	Illustrated guide to the geography of ancient England	913.620 022 2 or 913.620 4
9.	A gazetteer of Southern Africa	916.800 3
10.	Bahrain on $100 a day	915.365 04

EXERCISE 8.2

1.	A history of ancient Sparta	938.9
2.	A short history of the mountain regions of Bolivia	984.1
3.	Submarine warfare in the first World War	940.451
4.	The United States under President Ronald Reagan, 1981–1989	973.927
5.	A history of the Thirty Years war, 1618–1648	940.24
6.	The French Revolution	944.04
7.	The Russian Revolution	947.084 1
8.	History of the Persian Empire	935.05
9.	Norway in the 1950s: an outline history	948.104 3
10	The encyclopedia of Zambian history	968.940 03

EXERCISE 8.3

1.	Geology of Quebec	557.14
2.	Printmaking in Japan	769.952
3.	General statistics of Hungary	314.39
4.	Political conditions in the Irish Republic	320.941 7
5.	Economic conditions in Algeria	330.965
6.	Higher education in Vietnam	378.597
7.	Libraries in New Zealand	027.093
8.	The Roman Catholic Church in Paraguay	282.892
9.	Constitutional law of ancient China	342.31
10.	Life expectancy in Burundi	304.645 675 72

EXERCISE 8.4

1.	Snowmobiling in Scotland	796.940 941 1
2.	New Orleans brass bands	784.909 763 35
3.	Design and construction of buildings in Nagasaki	720.952 244
4.	Working mothers in ancient Rome	331.440 937 63
5.	Family counselling in Sweden	362.828 609 485

EXERCISE 8.5

The titles given are examples. Other titles covering the same topics are equally correct.

1.	942.052 007 2	Historical research on England in the reign of Henry VIII
2.	994.040 05	Journal of twentieth century Australian history
3.	306.743 094 93	Male prostitution in Belgium
4.	283.946	The Anglican Church in Tasmania
5.	372.9593	Elementary education in Thailand
6.	996.11	A short history of Fiji
7.	359.009 611	The Tunisian navy
8.	759.949 2	Painting and paintings of the Netherlands
9.	026.340 025 766 38	A directory of law libraries in Oklahoma County
10.	994.230 609 22	A history of famous South Australians since the 1960s

EXERCISE 8.6

1.	Raising pigs	636.4
2.	How to make soft toys	745.592 4
3.	Surfacing dirt roads	625.75
4.	Mobility of labour	331.127
5.	Problems providing food, clothing and shelter for those in need	361.05
6.	The encyclopedia of household pets	636.088 703
7.	Teaching drawing	741.071
8.	The theory of underwater photography	778.7301
9.	The philosophy of evolution	576.801 or 116
10.	Correspondence course in mathematics	510.715
11.	Radio in the 1930s	384.540 904 3
12.	The sociology of slavery in the Roman Empire	306.362 093 7
13.	Death customs in ancient Britain	393.093 61
14.	Theatre in Botswana	792.096 883
15.	Air pollution controls in Mexico	628.530 972
16.	Political parties in Peru	324.285
17.	Alligators of the Florida Everglades	597.983 097 593 9
18.	Gold mining in the Kimberleys of Western Australia	622.342 209 941 4
19.	Firefighting in South Australia	628.925 099 423
20.	Firefighting in the Flinders Ranges of South Australia	628.925 099 423 7

EXERCISE 8.7

1.	Modern archaeology: techniques and equipment	930.102 8
2.	The dictionary of place names	910.3
3.	Maps of Irian Jaya	912.951
4.	New South Wales during the Federation movement	994.403 2
5.	Scotland in the 1960s	941.108 56
6.	Ohio history quarterly	977.100 5
7.	The diplomatic history of World War II	940.532
8.	Exploration of Mars	919.923 04
9.	Lake fishing	799.109 169 2
10.	Marine transportation across the Atlantic Ocean	387.509 163
11.	Baboons of the grasslands	599.865 091 53
12.	Wind systems in valleys	551.518 5
13.	Paintings in the 17th century	759.046
14.	Ancient Egypt during the Middle Kingdom	932.013
15.	The Thai Historical Association journal	959.300 5
16.	Life expectancy in Spain	304.645 46
17.	Modern British philosophy	192
18.	Customs of Easter Island	390.099 618
19.	Dictionary of building	690.03
20.	Experimental research in pharmaceutical chemistry	615.190 072 4

EXERCISE 9.1

1.	American (in English)	81
2.	Dutch	839.31
3.	Swedish	839.7
4.	French	84
5.	Italian	85
6.	Catalan	849.9
7.	Portuguese	869
8.	Classical Greek	88
9.	Urdu	891.439
10.	Assamese	891.451
11.	Breton	891.68
12.	Slovenian	891.84
13.	Kota (Note that this is not a base number)	894.81
14.	Korean	895.7
15.	Xhosa	896.398 5

EXERCISE 9.2

1.	Poetry by an American poet	811
2.	A drama in Dutch by one author	839.312
3.	A collection of a Swedish novelist	839.73
4.	Short stories in English translation by a French author	843
5.	Letters written by a high-ranking Italian lady	856
6.	Speeches in Catalan by a famous politician	849.95
7.	A Portuguese author's miscellaneous writings	869.8
8.	Classical Greek poetry by a medieval poet	881.02

9.	20th century drama by an Urdu author	891.439 271
10.	A modern Assamese novel	891.451 372
11.	Letters by a 16th century Breton	891.686 1
12.	Speeches by a Slovenian citizen in 1920–1930	891.845 5
13.	Poems of a Kota woman	894.81
	(Do not add from Table 3 – this is not a base number)	
14.	Reminiscences of a Korean during the Yi period	895.782 03
15.	Xhosa fiction	896.398 53

EXERCISE 9.3

1.	The Penguin book of Chinese verse	895.11
2.	Fifteenth century English drama	822.2
3.	French essays between the World Wars	844.912
4.	A yearbook of Finnish literature	894.541 05
5.	Selected essays of Umberto Eco translated from the Italian (late 20th century)	854.914
6.	War and peace, a novel by Leo Tolstoy, translated from the Russian	891.733
7.	Mother Courage and her children, by Berthold Brecht, a tragedy translated from German, written 1936–1939	832.912
8.	Letters home: letters of Sylvia Plath, US poet, late 20th century	816.54
9.	Famous Greek ballads of the nineteenth century`	889.104 4
10.	The Spanish love story	863.085

EXERCISE 9.4

1.   A collection of poetry for children   821.008 092 82

    82   English language literature (schedules – base number)
      1 + 00   poetry (table 3B)
        80   collections of literary texts displaying features ...for ...
                      specific groups of people
          9282   for children (table 3C)

2.   An anthology of American poetry about animals   811.008 036 2

    81   American language literature (schedules – base number)
      1 + 00   poetry (table 3B)
        80   collections of literary texts ... emphasizing specific subjects ...
          362   about animals (table 3C)

3.   Poems by English women, Elizabethan to Victorian   821.008 092 87

    82   English language literature (schedules – base number)
      1 + 00   poetry (table 3B)
        80   collections of literary texts displaying features ...for ...
                      specific groups of people
          9287   by women (table 3C)

Note: the period is not included, since it is too broad

4.   An anthology of modern English drama   822.914 08
          82   English language literature (schedules – base number)
           2   drama (table 3B)
             914   1945–1999 (period table from schedules)
               08   collections of literary texts (table 3B: 'add' note under –21–29)

5.   A book of contemporary Latin-American short stories   863.010 886 8
          86   Spanish language literature (schedules – base number)
           301   short stories (table 3B)
             08   collections (table 3B : add as instructed under –102–107)
               8   literature ... by ethnic groups (table 3C)
                 68   Spanish Americans (table 5)

6.   Best sellers by French teenagers   843.009 928 3
          84   French language literature (schedules – base number)
           3   fiction (table 3B)
             009   standard subdivisions ... (table 3B: –3001–3009)
               9283   by teenagers (table 3C)

7.   A critical study of Manx literature   891.640 9
          891.64   Manx language literature (schedules – base number)
               09   history ... critical appraisal of works in more than one form (table 3B)

8.   Soviet literature of the 1980s : a decade of transition   891.709 004 4
          891.7   Russian language literature (schedules – base number)
             0900   history ... critical appraisal of works in more than one form (table 3B) –
                                  literature from specific periods
               44   1945–1991 (period table from schedules)

9.   The Virago book of ghost stories   823.087 33
          82   English language literature (schedules – base number)
           308733   ghost fiction (table 3B)

10.   The journal of Beatrix Potter from 1881–1897   828.803
          82   English language literature (schedules – base number)
           8   miscellaneous writings (table 3A)
             8   1837–1899 (period table from schedules)
               03   diaries (table 3A : from –81–89)

11. The grotesque in the arts 700.415
   700.4   Arts displaying specific qualities of style, mood, viewpoint (schedules – base number)
      15   grotesque (table 3C)

12. Comedy films 791.436 17
   791.4361   Films displaying specific qualities (schedules – base number)
      7   Comedy (table 3C: –17)

EXERCISE 9.5

1. The handmaid's tale, by Margaret Atwood (1939–)   C823.54 or C813.54 or 819.1354
2. The collected poems of Henry Lawson (1867–1922)   A821.2
3. Letters of Dame Kiri Te Kanawa (1944–)   NZ826.2
4. The Penguin book of great Canadian speeches   C825.008 or C815.008 or 819.150 08
5. The Oxford book of New Zealand melodrama   NZ822.052 708
6. Patrick White : a life, by David Marr (1947–)   A823.3

EXERCISE 9.6

1. Toronto writers' group anthology   C820.809 713 541
   C   Canadian literature (optional)
      82   English language literature (schedules – base number)
         080   Collections of literary texts in more than one form
               (table 3B: from –0801–0809)
            9   By residents of specific countries (table 3C: –93–99)
            713541   Toronto (table 2)

2. Australian women's writing   A820.809 287
   A   Australian literature (optional)
      82   English language literature (schedules – base number)
         080   Collections of literary texts in more than one form
               (table 3B: from –0801–0809)
            9287   by women (table 3C)

3. Seven Canadian holiday tales   C823.010 833 4
   C   Canadian literature (optional)
      82   English language literature (schedules – base number)
         301   Short stories (table 3B)
            08   collections (table 3B: from –102–107)
            334   holidays (table 3C)

4. New Zealand plays about monsters   NZ822.008 037
   NZ   New Zealand literature (optional)
      82   English language literature (schedules – base number)
         2 + 00   Drama (table 3B)
            80   collections (collections of literary texts emphasizing specific subjects)
            37   monsters (table 3C)

EXERCISE 10.1

1.	Mind your spelling (how to spell English words)	428.13
2.	Let's learn our ABC	correct
3.	A Chinese reader	495.186
4.	Street French : slang, idioms, and popular expletives (a historical approach)	correct
5.	A crossword dictionary	793.732 03

EXERCISE 10.2

1.	The Russian alphabet	491.711
2.	The history of Hebrew	492.409
3.	A new Lao reader	495.919 186
4.	Spanish pronunciation	468.13
5.	Modern German slang	437
6.	Speak standard Indonesian (for native speakers)	499.221 83
7.	Teach yourself Swahili (for non-native speakers)	496.392 824
8.	English Creole dialects of the Caribbean	427.972 9
9.	Conversational New Guinea Pidgin	427.995 3
10.	Portuguese as spoken in Brazil	469.798 1

EXERCISE 10.3

1.	A quick beginners course in Hindi for English speakers	correct
2.	Speak Greek in a week (for English speaking persons)	489.383 421
3.	Arabic phrase book (for English speaking persons)	492.783 421
4.	Fluent English for Danish speakers	428.343 981
5.	A Dutch-English dictionary	439.313 21
6.	A Japanese-German, German-Japanese dictionary	495.633 1

EXERCISE 10.4

1.	A French-Vietnamese dictionary	443.959 22
2.	A Khmer-English-Khmer dictionary	495.932 321
3.	Spanish words in the English language	422.461
4.	Serial publications in Tagalog	059.992 11
5.	Folk tales in Yiddish	398.204 391

EXERCISE 11.1

1.	Social anthropology of the Kurdish people	305.891 597
2.	Social anthropology of French Canadians	305.811 4
3.	Bedouin art	704.039 272
4.	Afrikaner folk music	781.623 936
5.	Social services to Catalans	362.844 9
6.	Metal engraving of Portuguese-speaking people	765.089 69
7.	Child rearing practices of the ancient Romans	649.109 37
8.	Polynesian football players	796.330 899 94
9.	Rum distilled by South American native people	641.259 089 98
10.	Palestinian Christians	270.089 927 4

EXERCISE 11.2

1.	Chemistry for potters	540.247 38
2.	The ethics of teachers	174.937 11
3.	Preschool children as artists	704.083 3
4.	The art of North American native peoples	704.039 7
5.	Aerodynamics for ornithologists	533.620 245 98
6.	Choreography for opera singers	792.820 247 821
7.	An anthology of poetry by well-known detectives	821.008 092 136 325
8.	Lesbian TV stars	791.450 866 43
9.	Eritrean cooking in Los Angeles	641.592 928 909 794 94
10.	Civil and political rights in Muslim countries	323.091 767

REVISION QUIZ 11.3

1. No, unlike the standard subdivisions of Table 1 (that can be added to any number as appropriate without instruction), notation from Tables 2 to 6 can only be added to a classification number when specific instructions are given in the schedules or in other tables.

2. Table 4 and Table 6.

3. (a) Follow specific directions in the schedules or in other tables, that instruct you to add notation from Table 2.
(b) If no specific instructions for adding notation from Table 2 are provided, add —09 from Table 1, then add the area notation from Table 2.

4. (a) Literature is classed first by original language (using the 800s), then by literary form, period and subject (using Table 3). In general, the rest of DDC classes first by subject, then by form.
(b) Table 3 is divided into three separate tables:
   Table 3A: works by or about individual authors
   Table 3B: works by or about more than one author
   Table 3C: additional notation for arts and literature, only used when needed
There is no other Table in DDC that is structured in this way.
Note: although the provision of options for emphasizing country-based literatures using the same language ('local emphasis') is a feature of the literature schedules, this feature is not unique to the 800s. Similar options appear in the 400s, although they are not used as often.

5. Table 5 represents groups of people, and lists notation for ethnic and national groups.

EXERCISE 12.1

The titles given are examples. Other titles covering the same topics are equally correct.

1.	940.316 2	Pacifists in World War I
2.	025.171 6	Managing collections of rare library material
3.	255.530 09	A history of the Jesuit order
4.	725.210 87	Design of shopping centres for disabled people
5.	782.107 941	British opera competitions

EXERCISE 12.2

1.	Financial journalists and journalism	070.449 332
2.	Snakes in the Bible	220.859 796
3.	Commerce in the Koran	297.122 838 1
4.	Conversion of non-Jews to Judaism in India	296.714 095 4
5.	Diseases in corn crops	633.159 3
6.	Restoration of commercial buildings	725.202 88
7.	Care of games in libraries	025.179 6
8.	Learning about crocodiles from museums	597.980 75
9.	Scientific works as literature	809.935 5
10.	Raising goats as stunt animals	636.391 8

EXERCISE 13.1

1.	A guide to coffee table design	749.3
2.	Growing begonias	635.933 627
3.	The law of income tax	343.052
4.	Aerial photography	(general) 778.35 or (military) 623.72
5.	Upholstering your sofa	(household) 645.4 or (design) 747.5
6.	Causes of unemployment	331.137 2
7.	Journalism in Moscow	077.31
8.	Modern British sheep breeds	636.32
9.	Modern art	709.04 (20th C) or 709.05 (21st C)
10.	Church architecture	726.5

EXERCISE 13.2

1.	Etruscan sculpture	733.4
2.	Dinosaurs	567.9
3.	Halley's comet	523.642
4.	A history of drug addiction	362.290 9
5.	Having twins : a parent's guide to pregnancy, birth and early childhood	618.25
6.	Chemical contraception	613.943 2
7.	Educating children with communicative disorders	371.914
8.	Sports injuries	617.102 7
9.	Fashion modelling	746.92 or (advertising) 659.152
10.	Bringing up children	649.1

EXERCISE 13.3

1.	The Crusades	correct
2.	The Apostles' Creed	correct
3.	Rhymes and rhyming games	398.8
4.	Xhosa language	496.398 5
5.	Forecasting storms	551.645

EXERCISE 14.1

The titles given are examples. Other titles covering the same topics are equally correct.

1.	005.382	Computer programs for specific operating systems
2.	070.593	Private publishers
3.	133.54	Horoscopes
4.	155.937	Death and dying
5.	268.67	Use of dramatic method in religious education
6.	303.484	Social innovation and change
7.	920.72	Biographies of women
8.	590.7346	Zoos of Spain
9.	428.42	Remedial reading
10.	423.15	Dictionary of acronyms and abbreviations
11.	509.2	Scientists
12.	428.405	A journal about reading
13.	658.45	Communication in management
14.	786.5092	Organists
15.	796.358 082	Women cricketers

EXERCISE 14.2

1.	Thailand: description and travel	915.930 4
2.	Central Australia: discovery and exploration (1795–1869)	919.420 42
3.	City of Adelaide (S.A.): description and travel in the 1930s	919.423 104 42
4.	Asia: description and travel in the 1980s	915.044 28
5.	Bahrain: travel in the twentieth century *(note: schedule instructions say 'do not add historical periods')*	915.365 04
6.	Natural monuments in Australia: a pictorial view	719.320 994
7.	The Readers' Digest guide to the coasts of Victoria, Tasmania and South Australia (designed to show points of interests in the 1980s)	919.404 64
8.	A guidebook for travel in Sydney	919.441 04
9.	A guidebook for travel in Colorado	917.880 4
10.	Geographic features of ancient Rhodes	913.916
11.	Travel in India during 318–500 AD	913.404 6
12.	Prehistoric geography of Carthage	913.973 01
13.	Maps of Yellowstone National Park	912.787 52
14.	Maps of the Hunter Valley of N.S.W.	912.944 2
15.	Atlas of the ancient world	912.3

EXERCISE 14.3

1.	Atlas of the oceans of the world	912.196 2
2.	Physical geography of mountains	910.021 43
3.	An illustrated atlas of islands	912.194 200 222
4.	Maps of the Pacific Ocean in the 18th century	912.196 409 033
5.	Maps of the ancient Roman Empire	912.37
6.	Spiritualism in Catholic countries	133.909 176 12
7.	Trade unions in Malaysia	331.880 959 5
8.	Social welfare services to the mentally ill in British Columbia	362.209 711
9.	A guide to the snakes of Ireland	597.960 941 5

10.	Rail passenger transport in Belgium	385.220 949 3
11.	Printmaking in France	769.944
12.	Water birds of the world	598.176
13.	Local government in the Southern Hemisphere	320.809 181 4
14.	Birds of the Indian Ocean	598.091 65
15.	A guide to wine making in New Zealand	663.200 993

EXERCISE 14.4

1.	Transplants in Transylvania	617.950 949 84
2.	The paintings of Tom Roberts	759.994
3.	Postage stamps of Angola	769.569 673
4.	Country music from Texas	781.642 097 64
5.	Horse racing tracks in Hong Kong	798.400 685 125
6.	Horse riding in the Australian Capital Territory	798.230 994 7
7.	Hunting in South Africa in the nineteenth century	799.296 809 034
8.	German Christian church architecture of the sixteenth century	726.509 43
9.	The Sydney Morning Herald & other Sydney newspapers	079.944 1
10.	Folk songs of Chile	781.620 098 3
11.	Dutch narrative poetry	839.311 03
12.	Spanish farce	862.052 32
13.	Twentieth-century Spanish drama	862.6
14.	The modern Indonesian novel – the works of Pramoedya Ananta Toer	899.221 32
15.	An Indonesian dictionary	499.221 3

EXERCISE 14.5

1.	English-Indonesian dictionary	423.992 21
2.	English-Indonesian-English dictionary	499.221 321
3.	Dictionary of Indonesian acronyms	499.221 315
4.	Use of French words in English	422.441
5.	English for Spanish people	428.346 1
6.	English for Malayalam-speaking people	428.349 481 2
7.	Choral singing for the hearing impaired	782.508 72
8.	Case histories in psychiatry	616.890 9
9.	Pasteur the chemist: a biography	540.92
10.	General biology: a quarterly magazine	570.5
11.	A guide to fascist political theory	320.533
12.	Harraps Russian dictionary	491.73
13.	The Roman Catholic Church in Spain	282.46
14.	The journal of sports medicine	617.102 705
15.	Kenya before the British	967.620 1

EXERCISE 14.6

1.	How to read maps	912.014
2.	Makeup for pantomime	792.302 7
3.	The ethics of euthanasia	179.7
4.	Biographies of ancient Egyptians	920.032
5.	Biographies of notable Canadians	920.071
6.	The movement for women's suffrage	324.623
7.	The Pankhursts: a biography of suffragettes	324.623 092 2
8.	Modern archaeology: techniques and equipment	930.102 8
9.	Genealogical sources of Scotland	929.341 1
10.	An introduction to historiography	907.2
11.	Aboriginal Dreamtime stories	299.9215
12.	Erotica in art	700.453 8
13.	Design of caravan parks for long-term residents	711.58
14.	An introduction to pumps	621.69
15.	Dictionary of biology	570.3

EXERCISE 14.7

1.	Dutch poetry of the 17th century	839.311 3
2.	The design of motels for the aged	728.508 46
3.	First aid for gunshot wounds	617.145 026 2
4.	Scotland under James II	941.104
5.	Modern joinery: a guide to Scandinavian practices	694.609 48
6.	The spiritual discipline of yoga	204.36
7.	Scale models of solar-powered automotive engines	629.221 95
8.	Manufacture of toilet tissue: patents	676.284 202 72
9.	Research in the engineering design of hand tools	621.908 072
10.	Underwriting health and accident insurance	368.380 12
11.	English fiction: a secondary school study guide	823.007 12
12.	The Bathurst prison riot	365.641 099 445
13.	Auckland Art Gallery	708.993 24
14.	The design of tug boats	623.812 32
15.	A zoological study of clams, mussels & cuttlefish	594

EXERCISE 14.8

The titles given are examples. Other titles covering the same topics are equally correct.

1.	549.911	Minerals of the polar regions
2.	513.071 2	Teaching arithmetic in secondary schools
3.	634.709 94	Growing berries in Australia
4.	853.914	Italian fiction since 1945
5.	912.9441	Sydney street directory
6.	978.1125	The history of Rawlins County
7.	025.065 786 809 946	Information storage and retrieval systems devoted to endangered species in Tasmania
8.	004.0151	Mathematical principles of computer science
9.	285.295 95	The Presbyterian Church of Vanuatu
10.	296.830 994 51	The history of the Jewish community in Melbourne

11.	305.488 992 109 4	Filipina women in Australia
12.	324.630 899 915	Elections for Aboriginal Australians
13.	338.274 309 959 2	Copper mining in Bougainville
14.	362.102 308 2	Women carers of people with physical illnesses
15.	378.33	International fellowships in higher education

EXERCISE 14.9

1.	Traditional Jewish rites: Bar mitzvah	296.442 4
2.	Research into the manufacture of synthetic perfumes	668.544 072
3.	Collecting pistols	623.443 207 5
4.	The waterfalls of Hawaii: a description	919.690 969 4
5.	Translating biochemical material	418.035 72
6.	Corals of the Australian Barrier Reef	593.609 943
7.	Canada under Trudeau	971.064 4 or 917.064 6
8.	The building of rock fill dams in the 19th century	627.830 903 4
9.	Nursing psychiatric patients	616.890 231
10.	Nebraska between the World Wars	978.203 2
11.	Residential care for heroin addicts	362.293 85
12.	Prostitution in the 20th century: a sociological study	306.740 904
13.	Photographs of animals	779.32
14.	Rotary clubs in Arizona	369.520 979 1
15.	The mining of tin	622.345 3

EXERCISE 14.10

The titles given are examples. Other titles covering the same topics are equally correct.

1.	181.07	Islamic philosophy
2.	153.947 96	Tests for sporting ability
3.	155.911 67	Psychology of taste
4.	428.340 709 4	Education and research in English as a second language in Australia
5.	331.124 15	Job openings in science
6.	331.137 810 274	Unemployment for public library staff
7.	331.119 166	Labor force in chemical engineering
8.	331.252 916 59	Pensions in advertising and public relations
9.	331.413 7	Female unemployment
10.	338.372 757	Trout as a product
11.	336.266 73	Import taxes on sculpture
12.	230.98	Shakers' doctrines
13.	220.52033	Concordance of the Bible (King James version)
14.	230.071 185	Higher education in Christian theology in Peru
15.	220.872 582 704 72	Energy conservation in amphitheatres in the Bible

GLOSSARY

This glossary contains terms used in *Learn DDC*. For a comprehensive glossary, see Farkas, Lynn, *LibrarySpeak: a glossary of terms in librarianship and information management*.

add To add in DDC means to attach or append a number to the end of another number—e.g., 636.825 + 39 = 636.82539

add note A note instructing the classifier to append (add) one number to another number

author number *See* book number

auxiliary table A table of numbers and/or letters that can be added to notation in the schedules to make a classification number more specific

base number The number found in the schedules of Dewey Decimal Classification to which a number can be added from the tables

book number The numbers, letters or combination of numbers and letters used to distinguish an individual item from other items with the same classification number

broad classification Classification using the main divisions and subdivisions of a scheme without breaking down into narrower concepts

built number A number not printed in the schedules, that is built by beginning with a base number and adding another number to it

call number A number on a library item consisting of a classification number, a book number and often a location symbol

caption Also heading. A name, word or phrase used to name a classification number

centered entry, centered heading A heading in Dewey Decimal Classification that applies to a range of classification numbers

citation order The order in which two or more aspects of a topic are combined in number building

class The broadest grouping of numbers in a classification scheme representing a subject group or discipline—e.g., religion

class-elsewhere note A note giving the classifier the location of related topics

classification A system for arranging library materials according to subject

classification number Number allocated to a library item to indicate a subject

classification scheme A particular scheme for arranging library materials according to subject—e.g., Dewey Decimal Classification, Library of Congress Classification

classified catalog A catalog where the entries are arranged in order of classification number

classify To allocate a classification number

close classification Classifying as specifically as possible, using all available subdivisions of a scheme

Colon Classification A classification scheme devised by S.R. Ranganathan for Indian libraries, using numbers and letters, and a colon to separate different parts of the classification number

complete revision A revision in which virtually all the subdivisions of a part of the schedule are changed

comprehensive number A number that covers all the aspects of the subject within a discipline

coordinate A number or topic at the same level as another number or topic in the same hierarchy. Cf subordinate, superordinate

copy cataloging Using an existing catalog record from a library or another source as the basis for one's own cataloging record, usually by copying the cataloging details and adding local location and holdings details

Cutter number A system of author numbers, devised by Charles A. Cutter, beginning with the first letter of the author's name and followed by numbers. Used in Library of Congress Classification for authors, titles and geographic areas

Cutter-Sanborn number An extension of the Cutter author number system, outlined in the Cutter-Sanborn Three-Figure Author Table. Designed to maintain works with the same classification number in alphabetical order of author

DDC *See* Dewey Decimal Classification

Dewey Decimal Classification (DDC) A classification scheme, devised by Melvil Dewey in 1873, using numbers to represent subjects

discipline A very broad group of subjects in a classification scheme—e.g., social science

discontinued number A number from the last edition that is no longer used. These numbers are shown in square brackets—e.g., [361.323]

division The second level of subdivision in Dewey Decimal Classification, represented by the first two digits of the notation—e.g., 51 in 510 Mathematics

enumerative classification Classification that attempts to spell out (enumerate) all the single and composite subjects required—e.g., Library of Congress Classification

EPC Dewey Decimal Classification Editorial Policy Committee. An international committee of experts that advises on the development of the Dewey Decimal Classification scheme

extensive revision A major reworking of some subdivisions, without altering the main outline of the schedule

facet An aspect or orientation of a topic

facet indicator A digit used to introduce notation representing an aspect, or facet, of a subject—e.g., the 0 in standard subdivisions like –09

faceted classification Classification that allows for notation to be built up by the use of tables and other parts of the schedules. All modern classification schemes are faceted to a degree. Colon Classification is the definitive faceted classification scheme

first-of-two rule The rule that requires a work covering two subjects in the same discipline to be classified at the number coming first in the schedules

first summary of Dewey Decimal Classification The 10 classes, each of which represents a broad discipline or group of disciplines

fixed location Items are labelled according to their physical location, rather than their intellectual content. Cf relative location

form 1. The way in which bibliographic text is arranged—e.g., dictionary. 2. Type of literary work—e.g., poetry, drama

form class Used for literature. Items are classified not according to subject, but according to their literary form—e.g., poetry, drama

form division Used for works on any subject that are presented in a particular bibliographic form—e.g., dictionary, periodical

generalities class, generalia class Used for very general topics and comprehensive combinations of topics—e.g., current affairs, general encyclopedias

heading Also caption. A name, word or phrase used to name a classification number

hierarchical classification Classification in which the division of subjects is from the most general to the most specific—e.g., Dewey Decimal Classification

hierarchy The ranked order of subjects in a classification scheme

including note A note enumerating topics that are included in the number but are less extensive than the heading. Standard subdivisions may not be added to the numbers for these topics

index 1. An alphabetical list of terms or topics in a work, usually found at the back. 2. A systematically arranged list that indicates the contents of a document or group of documents

interdisciplinary number A number covering a subject from the perspective of more than one discipline, including the discipline where the number is located

LCC *See* Library of Congress Classification

Library of Congress Classification (LCC) A classification scheme developed by the Library of Congress, using numbers and letters

literary warrant The volume of books written, or likely to be written, on a topic

location Where an item is housed. This can be the name of the library or the part of a collection

location symbol A symbol showing which collection an item belongs to—e.g., F for fiction

mixed notation A combination of types of symbol—e.g., numbers and letters used in Library of Congress Classification. Cf pure notation

mnemonic Aiding memory

notation The series of symbols that stand for the classes, subclasses, divisions and subdivisions of a classification scheme

number building Construction of classification numbers not listed in the schedules, following rules given in the scheme for combining numbers

option An alternative to the standard notation, provided to give emphasis to a particular aspect of a library's collection

phoenix schedule *See* complete revision

precedence order *See* preference order

preference order The order indicating which one number is chosen when there is more than one possible number representing different aspects of the topic

pure notation One type of symbol only – e.g., numbers – used as the notation of a classification scheme. Cf mixed notation

reduction Making a classification number shorter by omitting one or more groups of digits from the end of the number

relative index In a classification scheme, an alphabetical list of all topics and synonyms, showing the relation of the topics to all the disciplines they are associated with

relative location Items are classified in relationship to others depending on the subject. Cf fixed location

relocated topic A subject that has been given a different classification number

relocation Moving a topic to a new number in a new edition

revision An alteration of the text of DDC. There are 3 degrees of revision:
- *routine revision* – updating terminology, clarifying notes, providing modest expansions;
- *extensive revision* – a major reworking of subdivisions, without altering the main outline of the schedule;
- *complete revision* – virtually all the subdivisions of a part of the schedule are changed

routine revision Updating terminology, clarifying notes, providing modest expansions

rule of application The rule specifying that works about the application of one subject to a second subject are classified with the second subject

rule of three The rule specifying that a work giving equal treatment to three or more subjects that are all subdivisions of a broader subject is classified with the first higher number that includes all of them

schedule The enumerated classes, divisions etc. of a classification scheme, arranged in number order

scope note A note describing the range and meaning of a term or classification number, especially where the use of the number is broader or narrower than is apparent from the heading

second summary of Dewey Decimal Classification The 100 divisions, each of which represents a broad topic

see also reference A direction from one heading to another when both are used

see reference A direction from one heading that is not used to another heading that is used

segmentation The division of classification numbers into meaningful parts, with a view to abbreviating them for a particular library

shelflist The record of the works in a library in the order in which they are shelved

specific index In a classification scheme, an index with only one entry for each topic mentioned in the schedules

standard subdivision An auxiliary number in Dewey Decimal Classification that represents a standard form or treatment of a subject—e.g., –09 for historical treatment

standing room Where a topic does not have enough literature to have its own number. The topic is narrower than the number in which it is included, and number building is not allowed. This leaves open the possibility of adding a more specific number to a future edition

subdivision A section of a classification scheme or subject heading

subordinate At a lower or more specific level than another number or topic in the same hierarchy. Cf coordinate, superordinate

summary A listing of the main classes, divisions, sections or subdivisions, that provides an overview of the structure

superordinate At a higher or broader level than another number or topic in the same hierarchy. Cf coordinate, subordinate

synthesis The process of constructing a number by adding notation from the tables or other parts of the schedules to a base number

synthetic classification Classification that allows the classifier to construct (synthesize) numbers for composite subjects—e.g., Colon Classification, Universal Decimal Classification

table A set of numbers in a classification scheme that are added to a number from the schedules to make a more specific number

table of precedence *See* table of preference

table of preference A list of numbers indicating the order (preference order) in which they are to be chosen if all aspects cannot be included

third summary of Dewey Decimal Classification The 1000 sections, each of which is a whole number, and represents a specific topic

UDC *See* Universal Decimal Classification

unique call number A number on a library item consisting of a classification number, a book number and often a location symbol, that is different from every other call number in the library

Universal Decimal Classification (UDC) A classification scheme developed by the International Federation for Information and Documentation (FID) by expanding the Dewey Decimal Classification. It offers the most specific classification for specialized collections and is widely used in special libraries

work A term used in DDC to refer to any resource being cataloged. This differs from its use in RDA cataloging, where 'work' refers to the initial intellectual or artistic concept which eventually becomes a physical resource

BIBLIOGRAPHY

Chan, Lois Mai and Joan S. Mitchell, *Dewey decimal classification: principles and application,* 3rd edition, Dublin, Ohio, OCLC, 2003.

Cutter, Charles Ammi, *Cutter-Sanborn three-figure author table,* Swanson-Swift revision, Littleton, Colorado, distributed by Libraries Unlimited, 1969.

Dewey decimal classification and relative index, 23rd edition, edited by Joan S. Mitchell, Julianne Beall, Rebecca Green, Giles Martin and Michael Panzer, 4 volumes, Dublin, Ohio, OCLC, 2011.

Dewey services [OCLC – Products and services], Dublin, Ohio, OCLC [online]. Viewed April 2014
http://www.oclc.org/dewey

Taylor, Arlene, *Wynar's introduction to cataloging and classification,* revised 9th edition, Westport, Connecticut, Libraries Unlimited, 2004.

WebDewey, Dublin, Ohio, OCLC [online, by subscription].
http://dewey.org/webdewey/login/login.html

Wiegand, Wayne A., *Irrepressible reformer: a biography of Melvil Dewey,* Chicago, American Library Association, 1996.

INDEX

LEARN LIBRARY SKILLS SERIES

This series of paperback workbooks introduces skills needed by library science students and library technicians, as well as librarians seeking refresher materials or study guides for in-service training classes. Each book teaches essential professional skills in a step-by-step process, accompanied by numerous practical examples, exercises and quizzes to reinforce learning, and an appropriate glossary.

Learn About Information
International Edition ©2015
Helen Rowe
ISBN: 9781590954331 Paperback

Learn Basic Library Skills
International Edition ©2015
Helen Rowe and Trina Grover
ISBN: 9781590954348 Paperback

Learn Cataloging the RDA Way
International Edition ©2015
Lynn Farkas and Helen Rowe
ISBN: 9781590954355 Paperback

Learn Dewey Decimal Classification (Edition 23)
International Edition ©2015
Lynn Farkas
ISBN: **9781590954362** Paperback

Learn Management Skills for Libraries and Information Agencies
International Edition ©2015
Jacinta Ganendran
ISBN: 9781590954379 Paperback

Learn Library of Congress Classification
International Edition ©2015
ISBN: 9781590954386 Paperback

Learn Library of Congress Subject Access
International Edition ©2015
Lynn Farkas
ISBN 9781590954393 Paperback

Learn Reference Work
International Edition ©2015
ISBN: 9781590954416 Paperback

LIBRARY SCIENCE TITLES

LibrarySpeak:
A Glossary of Terms in Librarianship and Information Technology,
International Edition ©2015
Lynn Farkas
ISBN: 9781590954423 Paperback

My Mentoring Diary:
A Resource for the Library and Information Professions
Revised Edition ©2015
Ann Ritchie and Paul Genoni
ISBN: 9781590954430 Paperback

Quality in Library Service:
A Competency-Based Staff Training Program
International Edition ©2015
Jennifer Burrell and Brad McGrath
ISBN: 9781590954447 Paperback

TOTALRECALL PUBLICATIONS, INC.
1103 Middlecreek,
Friendswood, TX 77546-5448

Phone: (281) 992-3131
email: Sales@TotalRecallPress.com
Online: www.totalrecallpress.com